MW00779282

# The Year 2000 & After

## TORKOM SARAYDARIAN

*Visions for the Twenty-First Century*®

The Year 2000 & After

© 1991 The Creative Trust

ISBN: 0-929874-14-5
Library of Congress Catalog Number 90-90139

Printed in the United States of America

Cover design:        *Fine Point Graphics*
                     Sedona, Arizona

Printed by:          *Delta Lithograph, Co.*
                     Valencia, California

Published by:        **T.S.G. Publishing Foundation, Inc.**
                     *Visions For The Twenty-First Century* ®
                     P.O.Box 4273
                     West Hills, California 91308
                     United States of America

**Note:** The meditations and prayers contained in this book are given as guidelines. They should be used with discretion and after receiving professional advice.

# Table of Contents

*The sons of men are one*
*and I am one with them.*
*I seek to love, not hate;*
*I seek to serve*
*and not exact due service;*
*I seek to heal, not hurt.*


*Let pain bring due reward*
*of light and love,*
*Let the soul control the outer form,*
*And life, and all events,*
*And bring to light the love*
*That underlies the happenings of the time.*


*Let vision come and insight,*
*Let the future stand revealed.*
*Let inner union demonstrate*
*and outer cleavages be gone.*
*Let love prevail.*
*Let all men love.*

# 1

—•—

## *Toward the Year 2000*

In the Ageless Wisdom we read that a moment of great crisis is coming to this planet. The moment of crisis will be in May of the year 2000. The Tibetan Master, referring to this event, says that the highest center on this planet is going to release a fiery stream of energy toward humanity.

That stream of energy will create certain reactions and responses in humanity. He challenges all disciples from all races, all religions, and all traditions to be observant and prepare themselves for that moment of great crisis.

What will be the results when this energy is released? Great Sages say that there may be three results, depending on whether the majority of humanity reacts or responds to the energy.

First, there may be a slow degeneration. For example, the energy will be released to humanity, and humanity — with its poisons, pollution, hatred, malice, slander, and insanity — will slowly wipe itself off this planet.

We can see that pollution, hatred, and separatism are increasing everywhere. On the other hand, men and women of goodwill, peace, and vision are trying to overcome the separatism, pollution, destruction, and impurities and create a new world. But, if the majority of humanity does not respond to these energies, we will see after the year 2000 many malignant diseases slowly spreading all over the world. Insanity will be everywhere. We can already see a steady increase in crime in many cities throughout the world. The degeneration of morals is increasing. There may well be a slow pace of degeneration as humanity wipes itself off this planet.

Second, this energy may increase human free will to such a degree that a clash between the armed forces of the nations will be inevitable. This would mean a great war. If that war comes, all of our dreams and visions will evaporate because the planet would turn into a moon.

The third manifestation of this energy will be a result of our response to it. To respond means to contact this energy, have equipment to assimilate it, and slowly to manifest it creatively. Eventually we would create a life conditioned by our response to this energy. For example, if we start responding to this energy, the health of all nations will increase. Right human relations will be established. Peace will come on Earth. The Brotherhood of Humanity will be a reality, and people will respect and love each other. Perhaps, eventually, a unified humanity will be established, and members of humanity will feel that they are each other's brothers and sisters. Great freedom and love will emanate from their hearts. In this way we will make a great breakthrough into the New Age.

What will be the signs of the New Age?

*1. The inner potentials hidden within each of us will start manifesting themselves.* Man is a seed not yet bloomed. When human beings start blooming, they will be like great Masters and geniuses. There are treasures hidden within our heart, mind, and soul that have never manifested. To manifest these potentials, these possibilities within us, we need certain conditions. One of these conditions is that this certain great energy must pour into humanity. The second is that humanity must respond to that energy, assimilate it, and create those thoughtforms, ideologies, human relations, laws, and regulations that will help humanity see the path of its spiritual destination.

*2. Humanity will consider neighbors and friends to be more valuable than themselves.* Your neighbors and friends will be more important to you than yourself.

*3. The third manifestation will be an extreme purification of the mental plane.* Our minds are not pure yet. Most of us live in a sphere of fear, anger, hate, separatism, greed, jealousy, revenge, slander, and malice. All of these vipers are eating us. In the future, great psychiatrists and medical specialists will demonstrate and prove that fear eats our bones. Anger destroys our nervous system. Hatred destroys our brain and our liver. Jealousy damages our spleen. Slander destroys our thinking.

These vices have been manifesting for ages and ages. The result of this is a humanity which has brought itself to the edge of disaster. The release of this New Age energy can slowly create those thoughtforms, human relationships, and ideologies that will build the basis of right human relationships for the future.

We are going to prepare for this release of energy, even though the masses are not ready for it. Those people in the mass-consciousness who react to these incoming energies will slowly degenerate. Those who respond to these energies will regenerate themselves and survive. Survival of the fittest can be explained as the ability to respond to these new energies and be able to translate them in terms of pure, clear thinking and feeling, followed by right action.

Our entire life is a reflection of what we think and feel. Once we change our consciousness and thinking, our life will change.

How does our consciousness change and expand? Our consciousness changes, expands, and raises our beingness when we consciously respond to the energy released from the highest center. We cannot be enlightened about the true situation and the issues of life unless we consciously respond to that energy.

To prepare ourselves to respond to these energies, we are going to go through a specific discipline. This is the time of discipline. We have only a few years until the year 2000, and in these years we can do it. Even if only a small percentage of humanity responds to these energies, that percentage will act as receivers for this higher energy and be able to distribute it: first, through their own radiation; second, through their speech, writings, music, dramas, and through other creative works; third, through their thoughts; fourth, through organizing new laws and regulations and new visions. They will be proving to humanity that this is a better way to live. If we do not live in this new, creative way, we are preparing to destroy ourselves.

How will these energies be received? If you are angry and you receive these energies, you will use them to fuel your anger. If you hate people and this energy hits you, you will use it on the victims of your anger. If you are jealous, you will use the energy to strengthen your jealousy.

We must go through the process of purification before we will be able to receive the energy, assimilate it, and use it to increase our creative ideas, visions, thoughts, health, happiness, and success. This requires eight steps.

If you are conscious of the future, and you aspire toward the future, you are going to take steps now to change your life and be ready to receive these energies. Purification and preparation cannot be done in one or two days. It takes years of self-exertion.

*First, you must organize your mind.* To do this, you need to learn scientific meditation. Begin meditating three to five minutes daily. Eventually you can increase it to fifteen minutes daily. Meditation is very important because it organizes the mind, and it is the mind which will first contact that energy and which will produce a life for you according to the contents of your mental body.

Let us say that your mind is a garden, and in that garden are many weeds and poisonous plants. When the sun and rain hit these plants, you will see that your garden will produce more poisonous plants and weeds. But, if you have beautiful seeds in your mental plane such as solemnity, beauty, responsibility, love, respect, gratitude, forgiveness, aspiration, striving, great visions for humanity, and are making great efforts to overcome your personality and to contact a new vision, all the best seeds will start growing and blooming within your mind. Then you will have a field full of flowers.

What are the contents of your mind? If the mind is a garden full of weeds of hatred, jealousy, and greed, the energy will destroy you. If you have a garden where the sun or rain cannot reach, you feel safe because you know the weeds cannot increase. But once the rain, the sunshine, and the life-giving energies from Space hit your garden, you

will have two choices. You will either allow only the good
seeds to bloom, or allow your garden to be choked with
weeds. The weeds will control your life. To prevent such a
calamity, you are going to learn the science of meditation,
which is the art of planting good seeds.

Some esoteric and religious groups make meditation
very difficult to understand. Meditation is clear, scientific
thinking, reasoning, and logic. In meditation you take a
problem, look at it, and try to analyze it in such a way that
the result, the solution, is good for everyone including
yourself. This is sane, logical thinking.[1]

When you become a little more advanced in meditation,
you will start touching the *light* within you and making that
*light* shine upon your activities, feelings, and thoughts.

At a later stage of meditation, you will contact your
*Inner Guardian* and slowly think, feel, and act in the Light
of that Guardian.

In a more advanced stage of meditation, the *light* within
you will start *releasing and shedding* itself in all of your
thoughts, words, activities, and feelings.

These are progressive stages of meditation. Meditation
is not sitting and chanting mantrams. The meditation we
refer to is to sit and think. For example, in meditation, you
try to solve a mathematical problem, or solve a problem
existing between you and members of your family. You sit
and think with logic and reasoning. You try to find the best
solution. That is good meditation. Efforts to solve your
problems, and even the problems of others, through thinking will eventually prepare you to go to higher forms of

---

1. For further information regarding how to do meditation, please refer to the following
books: *The Ageless Wisdom, The Science of Meditation,* and *The Psyche and Psychism.*

meditation in which you use your innermost light to help humanity and other kingdoms.

*Second, in order to respond to that potent current of energy, you must purify yourself.* Whenever you start thinking about your friends or enemies, have pure thoughts that are helpful for them and for others. Pure thoughts are thoughts in which there is no fear, no anger, no hatred, no jealousy, no revenge, no slander, and no treason.

Sometimes we say, "If I do not think in terms of these seven vipers, how can I think?" You can observe that the majority of humanity is thinking in fear, anger, jealousy, hatred, revenge, slander, and treason. You are going to purify your thinking and feeling process. When you do this, your actions will reflect the degree of purity you have in your mind and heart.

The result of purification will be good health. When you have a contradictory thought in which your heart says, "You shouldn't do it," but you do it anyway, you have conflict.

If you can create peace within your heart and within your mind, your body will reflect that peace as health, energy, creativity, beauty, and vigor.

Start purifying your body. We have much poison in our liver, bones, and blood. You are going to find those medical and psychological means that can eventually purify your system from the pollutants that you have put in it. If your body is purified, your thinking will be clearer. Your feelings and relationships will be more positive. Why not purify your body? Do not increase poisons in your body by eating wrong foods, drinking wrong things, and having wrong relationships with people.

The body must be purified. When the energy hits a body which is not "together," the result will be destruction. For example, there was a young man using marijuana and other drugs for ten years. Finally he came to his senses and said to me, "I want to do meditation and serious study. I want to save myself and be a great initiate." My first response to him was, "Take it easy. For many years you have destroyed your brain, nervous system, and poisoned your aura. Doing meditation will release from within you a heavy voltage of electricity which will hurt you. It will damage your whole nervous system." I suggested that he clean his diet and not use any drugs. I advised him to read and listen to lectures sparingly and take it easy for a few years. Then, after he had healed his body, I would give him the first steps of meditation.

He did not like this. He wanted to be a Master immediately so that everyone would worship him. He did not know that, as one advances and becomes a Master, his pain and suffering increase.

The young man went to a "master" who told him, "This is the time of salvation. Start meditating for forty minutes daily." The man's mother called me a few months later saying that her son was in an asylum. When energy is released into our system, and we are polluted and intoxicated, it activates the poison in our system and causes trouble for us.

Sometimes our body is strong and our aspiration is so deep that we pass through certain dangers but pay heavily in the future.

Purification is very important, and you are going to start purifying yourself. For example, purify your speech. To purify the speech is so difficult, especially when someone suddenly steps on your "tail." You say a few words, then think, "Well, purification didn't work." You must slowly purify your expressions, but primarily you must purify your thinking.

*Third, create a new image of yourself.* Each of us has an image of "I am that person." That image is built primarily of our failures, disappointments, and defeats. We look at ourselves as something rotten. When we are with people, we pretend that we are beautiful. But when we are alone, we feel that we are rotten people because we have a negative image of ourselves and we cannot ignore it. Because we are stuck to that past image of failure, defeat, ugliness, and memories of transgressions, we build an image and think, "I am not worthy. Who am I?" In our lonely moments we see this image. Such an image slowly molds our future. We cannot have a successful, victorious, triumphant future as long as that image is controlling our mind and life.

The image we are referring to is like a small photographic negative. We can shine a light behind the film and project the image onto a screen. If you have an ugly image, it is revealed in detail. This is why when you start meditating and aspiring and doing your best in everything, you sometimes feel that you are a rotten person. The only thing that makes you happy is that you think no one else sees it! This ugly image in your mind is going to be broken.

How will you break this image? The Tibetan Master gave a mantram. He suggested that every day at noon we recollect ourselves, focus our consciousness and say,

> *More radiant than the sun,*
> *purer than the snow,*
> *subtler than the ether*
> *is the Self,*
> *the Spirit within my heart.*
> *I am that Self,*
> *that Self am I.*

Regardless of what you have done or what people think about you, you are a Spark of God. Increase that thought within you. Think about this to such a degree that eventually you feel that you really are that Self. Do not worry about how much you have been defeated, or how many times you have failed! Do not worry about how much wrong you have done! Do not identify with these events. **You are a child of the Almighty Creator**. Put this image in your mind instead of an ugly image you have built of yourself. Until you change that old image, there is no hope for your progress.

You hear people say, "I shouldn't have done that. How did they defeat me? I am a defeated person. I am hopeless and penniless," etc. As long as you think about yourself in that way, and as long as you identify yourself with your failure and defeat images, you cannot go forward. You are going to say, "Who cares what people think about me or what I think about myself! I am going to improve and transcend myself."

People petrify your image and condense it to such a degree that even when you try to get out of that image, they do not let you. For example, they say, "Don't you know that you are a prostitute?" They repeat it again and again until they make a woman believe that she is. But if she decides to work against that image and starts saying, "More radiant than the sun. Wow, I can be so beautiful," then there will be hope.

This is demonstrated in one of Buddha's stories. A very bad woman went to see Buddha. His disciples stopped her and said, "Who are you to want to see the Buddha?"

But she said, "No matter what, I am going to see Him."

They said, "Woman, everyone knows about you and what you are."

She replied, "It does not matter; I am going to see Him." She went before Buddha and asked, "Lord, is it possible to save myself?"

"Oh yes," He replied, "it can happen in one moment. Imagine what you want to be and you will be it."

She suddenly imagined that she was a great Buddha sitting on a lotus. The story says that she immediately changed into a Great Tara and sat on a lotus.

Then Buddha said, "Each of you, in one second, can destroy the image that you had and be something great."

You are not advancing because your old image is still in your mind. Take that image away. You think in terms of your past failures, defeats, ugliness, and other bad things that you did. Get rid of such images and find a new way. Build a new image. Strive to improve yourself.

You can build a new image of yourself by visualizing yourself as beautiful as you can imagine. I remember a psychiatrist saying to me, "I came to say good-bye. I am going to the other world."

"Oh, are you going to commit suicide?"

"Yes," he replied.

"What is your reason?" I asked.

"For fifty years I have been in this profession. People's pain, suffering, and problems are embedded in my head. Suddenly I saw that I am one of them — a rotten person. Can you imagine, for fifty years I have been earning one hundred dollars an hour, and I have never helped these people."

"Oh, that is fantastic. You have learned many things. Close your eyes."

"Are you going to hypnotize me?" he asked. "Absolutely not!" I said. He closed his eyes.

I said to him, "Imagine that you are very happy, sitting in a meadow. There are beautiful flowers everywhere. Then imagine that you have found a beautiful woman. The two of you are dancing and singing."

I was slowly changing his image of himself. Later I changed him into a man who saved two or three people from drowning in a river. His face showed that he was jumping into the river and pulling them ashore. Eventually, I had him save a nation and bring humanity into peace. He became greater and greater.

"You rascal," he said to me, "now I don't want to die."

"What are you going to do?" I asked.

"I don't have much time left, so I must start working for these great visions." He is now so happy.

Trouble started when he became so happy. His wife called and asked me, "What did you do to this man? He is insane." According to his wife, he was not insane when he was trying to destroy himself, but he became insane when he started to save himself and others.

The third step, then, is to change your image. I know that you do not like yourself. You have many weird images of yourself. Think about the opposite of these images. For example, you have failed in something and that failure is really killing you. Let us say that you lost tens of thousands of dollars. That is a thoughtform registered in your brain. It is going to "eat" you. Day and night you are thinking in terms of your failures. If you plan for future successes, these past defeats and failures will come and say, "Hey, you failed. Do not try again because the same thing will happen."

How can you defeat this image? You can defeat it by first visualizing the whole process of your failure and defeat and then changing it into success. Regarding the people who stole your money, visualize and impose on your negative thoughtform that these people are bringing you millions of dollars. Take it and feel it in your hands. Take the money to the bank and buy properties. Make the visualization so fantastic that eventually the defeat thoughtform is itself defeated.

You will find this to be very practical. The transformation will not occur in one or two moments. You are going to be like a "crazy" person and say, "I am going to be successful at least in my dreaming and visualization." Once you do this, you will see that the negative images which are sapping your energies will get weaker and weaker until you finally conquer your old failure image and build a new image of success.

One day, two young teen-age brothers said to me, "No girls want to look at us. It is very painful for us. We smile at them, but they turn away." I knew their parents. The moment the boys would open their mouths, the parents would say, "Why are you speaking, walking, eating in such ugly ways?" These two boys had an ugly image of themselves and also that no girl could be interested in them.

When the boys changed their image, they became magnetic. Defeat images, failure images, and ugly images make you repulsive. When you change your image, you become positive. You not only attract men and women, you also attract money, success, and friends who will help you in every way possible.

*Fourth, radiate goodness.* Every day, do good for someone. For example, write a letter to someone who needs your encouragement. It can be a very small gesture.

Whenever you are caught in one of your own problems, think about someone else, someone who may be in a hospital. Call or write that person and say, "Hey, you will be all right," even if you are crying the next moment. That does not matter. You are going to do these acts of goodwill. Radiate goodwill and goodness. If someone is depressed, if someone is in pain, in separation or divorce, it is your place to be with him. Tell him that things will be better in the future. Say to him, "I love you. Even if no one else loves you, I really love you." Such goodness prepares your aura in such a way that it becomes magnetic to receive and respond, in some degree, to the Shamballa energy which will be released in the year 2000.

Forgiveness is also part of this fourth step. Let us say that something happened between you and another person. Why have you not been speaking to each other for three or four years? Why have you been gossiping, slandering, and increasing malice against each other? Forget such things. Go hug that person and say, "Let's forget about that incident. So what! Let's create a new relationship." This will increase your creative energies and your magnetism. When your magnetism and creative energies increase, they will bring things to your life to use for your success and for your victories.

These are new ways of living that you must impose upon your old life patterns.

Try to radiate goodness. Maybe someone says to you, "Do you know that silly girl who hated and slandered you for the past five years? She had an accident and died." You might say, "I knew that karma would hit her some day. In the next incarnation she will be a donkey because she hurt me." Instead, you are going to say, "I am really sorry now. I used to love that girl. I know how her friends and family must feel. I am so sorry. May God bless her." In doing this, you are changing your negative expressions to positive expressions. You are radiating goodwill instead of destructive energy. Whatever energy you manifest, that energy returns to you. Destructive energy destroys you. Constructive energy builds you. You must be very careful how you use the energy.

*Fifth, think about humanity as if humanity were one great family.* We have many cleavages; we hate and love many races, religions, and traditions. Regardless of what people and groups are on the outside, you are going to focus your consciousness on their Essence. In essence, all humanity is the manifestation of God.

> *I seek to love, not hate.*
> *I seek to serve*
> *and not exact due service.*
> *I seek to heal, not hurt.*[2]

If you say this in your mind and start motivating and programming yourself, you will be very successful, happy, healthy, and prosperous.

At the beginning of the year 2000, you must be a transformed person. Do not think that transformation is far away from you. It is just a matter of purification of your thinking, purification of your heart, and purification of your activities. When you do these, you will be the seed of the new race.

The new race will be tremendously creative. People's psychic energies will start developing. They will create new relationships with Higher Worlds and come in conscious contact with those Great Ones Who are directing the energies of the Universe. Try to build and synchronize yourself with that vision.

---

2. Mantram of Unification. For explanation, please see *Five Great Mantrams of the New Age*, p. 23.

# $Q_{\&}A$

**Question:** *In building a good image, how do you avoid building vanity?*

**Answer:** When our glamors or illusions build our self-image, it becomes charged with vanity. But if we build high standards for ourselves and try to achieve them, we do not build vanity because we strive, and at the same time we see where we are. Reality annihilates vanity, if we have vision.

Generally, vanity is imposed upon us by those who seemingly love us. They say, "You are so pretty." You then start thinking that you are outstandingly pretty and use their image of you to cheat them and others.

Suppose a weight lifter begins by lifting one hundred pounds. He then says, "Next year I am going to lift one hundred and fifty pounds." Working toward lifting one hundred and fifty pounds, when done rationally, logically, and in sane ways, does not build vanity. You are putting projects and visions in front of you and striving toward them. Vanity does not create striving because vanity says, "You are already a great one." One is a challenge to achieve. The other is an imposition on your mind that you are already there.

**Question:** *Where does ego fit in?*

**Answer:** Ego says, "Everything is for me. There is nothing for others. Everyone must serve me, respect me, and bring things to me. Everyone must cherish me, bribe me, and praise me," etc. You become the center of everything. It is a false center, a whirlpool that slowly, slowly swallows you, and you lose your identity. Ego is a false image about yourself. You did not plan to build it. It is already built through your lies, your hallucinations, and your daydreaming. It is also built through what people say about you. People build your ego. You do not build your ego all by yourself.

Ego is a false image imposed upon you by your glamors, illusions, vanity, and ignorance. When you are sane, you say, "I want to be beautiful." You then dress beautifully, you make your hair beautiful, etc. On the other hand, if you make yourself ugly and say that you are beautiful, this is vanity. One is a challenge; the other is acceptance that you are already beautiful.

> **Question:** *In the year 2000 when the energies come in, since we are so intertwined with humanity, it seems like some will respond and most will react. What should we do in this case?*

**Answer:** We do not know what the situation will be. As this age is coming to an end, the Teaching is increasing. Great pieces of literature and warnings of the dangers are coming to the surface. Many disciples are appearing. Many potential disciples, who were hidden under their glamors and illusions, are awakening and seeing the situation. For example, I recently read several unique articles in a local paper exposing many forms of poisons and pollution that have been used in our water, meat, fruits, and vegetables. People are awakening. Maybe humanity will suddenly awaken and say, "Hey, this is crazy. What have people been doing to us?" We are more aware of the poisons in our foods than we were five years ago. There can be a sudden awakening. Not all of humanity is yet awakened.

The impact of the Shamballa energy will not be drastic if three or four million disciples stand together. They will change the condition of life on this planet. Light is stronger than darkness. Even if we darken a large temple, we can destroy the darkness with only a few matches or candles.

Have faith. It creates a bad image if we say that darkness is powerful, evil is powerful, corruption is powerful. They are not. If we say that they are, we are accepting and energizing them. We are not going to accept that image. Evil always destroys itself. We have seen this throughout history.

> **Question:** *Do you prophesy a reasonably stable international situation between now and the year 2000?*

**Answer:** To be honest, who am I to answer that question? My feeling is that there are great signs that the world is going toward understanding and peace. I am seeing this. We are either going to destroy ourselves, or we are going to live together. Nations are going to realize this. The best way is to come together and enjoy life instead of destroying each other. This idea is spreading. Great leaders are realizing this and even teen-agers know about it. It is not a secret.

Still, some people are attached to their old images of war, hatred, destruction, and victory through conquering and killing. That is such an ugly image. Who knows from where it originated. The image of being victorious over others is a large pollutant in the mind of humanity. We must begin to say, "We are going to be victorious over our own weakness, not victorious over others."

Disciples will speak and write about these concepts. This is not the time to accumulate money, property, and higher positions. Your money and property are going to be devastated and turned into ashes if you do not put all your efforts into changing the thinking of humanity. In the New Testament a man said, "Wow, I have so much to eat and to wear." Then he turned to himself and said, "Hey, drink, eat, and be happy." Suddenly a little angel whispered in his ear, "Today you are going to die." What will remain? Humanity is now at that moment. You must work for the salvation of the world. Do not even work for the salvation of yourself.

Do everything possible. If you have money, use it now to spread these ideas. If you are in an influential position, speak. If you are creative, write new dramas and movies that will change the consciousness of humanity and save it. If you do not save humanity, you will be sinking. To save yourself, you are going to save the whole boat. Jumping into the ocean to save yourself will not do it.

**Question:** *How can we make the year 2000 a significant date?*

**Answer:** First, you are going to make that date significant with your preparation and your readiness to absorb these incoming energies. If you start absorbing these energies and responding to them, after the year 2000 a new way of thinking, feeling, and human relations will begin. It is you who will make it significant. If people do not make it significant, the energy will come in any case and the result will be widespread insanity. The statistics are very frightening. In the last ten years there was a fifty percent crime increase in many cities. Today, in certain areas, the increase in crime is over two-hundred and fifty percent. In some cities you cannot walk outside after dark. The quality of a college education in some areas is going backward. Crime, gangs, and drugs are increasing.

The day that humanity will take decisive action to stop these crimes all over the world will be a very significant day. These crimes are hurting humanity. For example, a silly young man drives his car under the influence of drugs and kills five people in an accident. Several police cars come. Fire engines come to the scene and stay for a few hours. Your taxes increase every year. You are paying for every crime, and you are sharing in all the pollution. This must be stopped. If you have money, find ways and means to put money into the hands of those who can use it to prevent the destruction of humanity.

People in general are still sleeping and they do not know what is going on. If they were really awake, they would see that the situation is very frightening.

We are going to take steps to strive toward changing ourselves and changing our friends. If possible, we must speak internationally and say that many of our present attitudes and approaches to solving problems are not the way to save humanity. For example, if the ozone disappears a little more, we will see a widespread increase in cancer, brain diseases, and various other problems. Some nations have refused to help correct the situation for another ten or fifteen years because it will hurt their economy. Others are working to prevent further damage. Let the economy be hurt. Human lives must be saved. This kind of thinking must be spread.

> **Question:** *Will you address the issue of drugs and how entire countries operate on the profits of drugs? It affects all of us. How can we correct this?*

**Answer:** We can provide such countries with new plans and alternative ways to make money. For example, if I had the power, I would go to those countries that are providing millions of tons of drugs to others and say, "How much money are you making daily?" "Two million daily." "Okay, let's build a great bridge, build a great hospital, plant a forest, and I will pay for it." Remember, we must build for humanity and for ourselves.

Money must be used in the right way. But we do not have such thinkers or leaders. Instead, we destroy people and throw them into prison. Then their successors do the same thing. We are not healing the problem from its roots. We are trying to heal the leaves when it is the roots that are sick.

Another way is to boycott all exports from such a country. The best way to bankrupt corrupt groups and nations is not to encourage them with our money. But if they have a certain number of customers in this country, they will survive. Unfortunately, we are pouring millions of dollars into countries that are selling drugs.

We are going to educate our citizens, especially our children, not to buy drugs. Then the problem will stop. Our government is now putting great energy and money into the fight against illegal drugs. Drugs are the number one enemy for this country.

Quite honestly, in the thirty years that I have been counseling, approximately six thousand young people have stopped using drugs. I did this without taking any money from the government, without any special funds. Thousands of people who were heavy drug users are now "diamonds" and "pearls." If I did this, you can do it, too. I just talked with them, saying for example, "Drugs are not good for you. See what is happening to your life."

Once twelve people came to my home to argue with me that marijuana is good to use. I said, "Okay, I will show you." They were all college students, so I gave them a few simple algebra problems to solve, but they could not do them. I said to them, "If your life brings you to a critical stage where you must think in order to survive and you cannot do this, you will lose yourself." The problem of these twelve young people is a symbol of the larger problem of international drug use.

We must find the reason and logic to tell them why using drugs is bad, and it must be done without punishment and imprisonment. Imprisonment does not help. Those who take drugs are already in prison. Recently, two people were released from prison after being there for five years. I asked them what they were going to do. They replied, "We hate the authorities. We are going to use and sell drugs again." The several thousand dollars that we spent imprisoning them did not help them. We are going to find out how to transform them into their Essence and, lovingly and with goodwill, save their minds.

> **Question:** *Did you say that the way to purify the emotional body is first to purify the mental body?*

**Answer:** Purification must be handled in three ways at once. There is not a separate first, second, and third way. If you are purifying your mind and drinking poison, purification does not work. If you are eating very well, but hating all day, purification will not occur. All three personality vehicles must be purified together. They are interconnected. Each of them is affected by the actions of the others. You are going to work in a three-dimensional way by purifying your activities, feelings, and thinking simultaneously.

> **Question:** *Will we reach a point at the year 2000 where the large number of homeless people, child abuse cases, and drug problems, etc. will be corrected if we just purify ourselves?*

**Answer:** To the degree that you purify yourself, by three times that amount you help others. But if you are not integrated, how can you cause others to be integrated? You must bring yourself together in order to cause togetherness in others. The first labor is to purify yourself. Understand your problems and find the ways and means to solve them.

Then, when you reach the stage of helping others, you can do it. Doctors, in their first year of training, do not try to perform surgery, but they make themselves ready to perform surgery.

Unfortunately, many of our universities are teaching wrong motives, for example, "Be a doctor in order to make a large annual salary." They do not say, "Be a doctor so that you can serve people day and night and maybe not make a lot of money." Perhaps you will find a few doctors like that.

You are going to prepare yourself to help, and in the meantime, to the degree that you are prepared — through purification — to that degree you can start helping. I remember a teen-ager who stopped taking drugs, then talked with two or three others and convinced them to stop using drugs. At her level, she was successful. If you want to serve more complex and greater levels, you must prepare yourselves. Five hippies said to me one day, "We are going to save this nation." I asked them, "How are you going to save this nation if you aren't even ready to save yourselves?"

The challenge is here. Know as much as you can. Be as much as you can. Have as much as you can so that you have something to give to people, teach people, and lead people. You are going to be strong and jump into the water to save the drowning ones. Prematurely trying to help others will create disturbances in them, and you risk your life.

One day my father brought home a very nice clock. I was seven years old and very curious about the mysterious thing that was going on inside the clock. So I disassembled everything. My mother asked what I was doing. I replied, "I am repairing the clock." "Oh all right, continue." The pieces were everywhere. When the time came to reassemble them, I could not do it. My father said, "What have you done?" I said, "I was curious to see what was inside." "But you were not able to put them back together. Why did you disassemble them?" In this way, people give wrong advice to others. One girl tells another, "If you want to be healthy, swallow five hundred pills." Everyone wants to appear as a philosopher or doctor!

We need preparation. The best preparation is to try to change our image. From now on start loving yourself. Say, "I am a Spark of God. I love myself. I am going to release the Divine Beauty conceived within me, and next year people are going to see how beautiful I am."

> **Question:** *I noticed that some spiritual groups occupy themselves with arguments and do not work for the substance. What do you think the reason is?*

**Answer:** Let me tell you a story. Twenty-one members of a religious group used to sit and discuss the words of the Bible.

One day, the topic was, "Is the Holy Spirit an emanation from God, from the Son, or is it a self-emanated power?" The people were divided into three sections, and each section was very serious and attached to its own opinions. After a six-hour debate, no group agreed with the other, and there was no conclusion. They left the room in anger and disappointment.

For years these group members never spoke to each other, but at every opportunity they slandered each other and tried to talk about the others' personal weaknesses. Eventually, they became each other's enemy.

Once I asked my Teacher if he could analyze why such things occur. He said, "**First of all,** the people were not ready to discuss such topics before their personalities were purified of anger, hate, slander, etc.

"**Second,** their intention was not to discover the truth, but to impose their opinions upon each other in order to gain superiority. So they were not freed from their ego.

"**Third,** they did not know that by discussing the Holy Spirit, they were attracting the energy of the Holy Spirit to their nature, and stimulating or energizing both their vices and virtues. And because their vices were more abundant than their virtues, they had devastation in their relationships with each other.

"**Fourth,** the group members stayed together to protect their crystallized opinions and save their faces.

"**Fifth,** whenever people are not ready to understand and actualize lofty ideas, they take revenge on each other — through various means and forms."

After these five points, my Teacher looked into my eyes and said, "Now, you find the **sixth** reason for their behavior." I asked his permission to bring my answer to him in a few days.

For days I thought about the event and finally came to the conclusion that they were debating about the chemical construction of fire, but were not interested in using the fire for their transformation.

They wanted to know where the fire came from, before cooking their breakfast. I thought that this was a good discovery, and I went to my Teacher and said, "I think I have some insight into the matter, but I feel it is not the whole answer," and I presented my discovery to him on a sheet of paper. He read it a few times, and eventually said,

"It is very good. Let me add the **seventh** reason. Every group member hated the others because none had the light and wisdom to pull out of the others their crystallizations and mental formulations and to make them taste what the Holy Spirit is. So they felt deprived."

One day a Communist and a Christian were debating in anger and an old man was listening to them. The Communist was saying, "We will make the whole world a Communist world." The Christian was saying, "We will make all the world Christian." After they were both exhausted, the old man said, "You, the Communist, can you honestly tell me if you are satisfied with the results of Communism?"

The answer was, "Of course, not." "And you, Christian, can you tell me that Christians all over the world are living according to the ideals Jesus presented?" "No." "Then I have some advice for you. Try to find what the purpose of life is, and try to discover a way that can lead us to that purpose, especially if both Communism and Christianity have failed." After a pause, he continued, "I am not advising you to bring theories to me — but actualization. I mean, you must demonstrate in your life the way that you think will lead us to our ultimate purpose — Home."

# 2

—•—

## *Discipleship in the Year 2000*

There is a law in the Universe which emanated from the Core of the Creator in the Universe. This law deals with the tendency to build units. Imagine the creation of the world from a homogeneous energy field. We can see scientifically, philosophically, and religiously that this energy is used to build units. For example, atoms are aggregations of energy, or condensations of energy. There are cells which are also units. There are various forms in nature, such as animal, vegetable, and human forms. Within humanity, there are family units. There are groups and nations. There is now a tremendous tendency in the Universal Field to challenge nations into unity. The United Nations is becoming a magnet to unite all nations.

A unity is starting to compose itself in our minds which says, "There is not only humanity; there are also animals, trees, vegetables, mountains, and rivers that are part of us." We are coming to unity-consciousness. The Universal

Consciousness is building concepts of unity within us — units within units. Eventually this concept will expand and we will see that man will feel as if he were the Globe and the Solar System. And later we will feel that the whole Universe is nothing but a unit. Philosophers have referred to this concept as the microcosm and the macrocosm. Man is the microcosm reflecting the macrocosm. The macrocosm is the rhythmic, orchestrated, "symbolic" whole Creation — the Cosmos. We are micro-cosmoses.

The Solar System is a unit created by the Universal Energy. The Solar System is a complete unit orchestrated in such a way that you cannot add to or subtract from it. It is a unit. The Solar System reflects the Galaxy, and the Galaxy reflects the Whole. We are reflecting the Earth and the Solar System. Our Solar System has its head, heart, stomach, legs, hands, etc. If you understand the man, you will also understand the Solar System.

Man has seven centers and the Solar System has seven centers. Certain planets act as centers for the Solar System. When we think more deeply about the concept of units, we reach a very subtle understanding that units cannot be composed if the smaller units within a unit do not act in right ways toward each other. Somewhere, the units composing a group are going to adjust themselves by subtracting from or adding to themselves in order to fit in the orchestra, but without losing their individuality.

In a musical score there are hundreds of measures, notes, pauses, flats, and sharps. These elements are organized in such a way that they increase each other's glory and beauty without hindering the manifestation, the expression, of each note and each instrument in the symphony. This is how a symphony is created.

The symphony is a great symbol of right human relations. The notes are organized in such a way that they do not hinder each other. On the contrary, they add to each other so that each shines, manifests, and expresses itself to its maximum capacity and thus contributes to the whole symphony.

When we refer to right human relations, we are also thinking, in the deeper layers of our mind, that units can be composed, can be healthy, and can be in expanding, progressing positions if the little units composing the greater units are conscious of their duties, responsibilities, place, and relationship with the other units.

On the path of the orchestration of all these units, there are small "fleas" and "rabbits" that jump forward and backward, right and left. They spoil the balance and harmony and create disturbances in the formation of the groups, the units. These "fleas" are self-interest, vanity, ego, mine and yours, show-offs, and "I am somebody. You must listen to me," etc. You are going to imagine that every obstacle and every hindrance on the path of forming groups is eventually crushed under the Wheel of that great Law which builds units. This great Law is against every kind of isolation and separatism.

For millions and millions of years that Universal Wheel, the tendency to create units, rolled until energy turned into atoms. The atoms then became cells, then organisms, then bodies, and so forth.

Every obstacle and hindrance on the path of that rolling Wheel is destroyed. We know this because we can see the result in our bodies. The physical body is an example of that Law. For millions of years, due to that Law, the human body has conquered hindrances and perfected itself.

When we say that our body is healthy, this means that there are right relations in that body. The stomach is not saying, "Who cares about the heart?" The kidneys are not saying, "To hell with this body; we want to grow by ourselves." Other cells are not saying, "We don't care about this body. We want to grow in our own way." When cells go their own way, they produce tumors and cancer.

There are tumor groups, tumor nations, and tumor companies. These are units acting like tumors. But if you examine history, you will see that the Great Wheel eventually grinds them and gradually creates a nation, a United Nations, one humanity, one Solar System, one Galaxy. How was the Galaxy created? It was created under that magnetic, radioactive Will, the Law that creates units.

One of the most sacred Laws is the Law of Right Human Relations. Right human relations leads to the Glory of God. The Glory of God manifests through you if you exercise right human relations within your group, nation, and within the Universe.

Anyone acting against the formation of right human relations is condemned to be destroyed eventually with his own karma, with his own deeds, with his own separatism. That Law is the supreme Law that grinds everything that comes under Its Wheel.

Buddha said, "If anyone in my group or in my Brotherhood brings any degree of separatism, he or she must immediately leave." He never accepted any element that created disturbances. He taught that the greatest cardinal sin is separatism. That sin is against the greatest laws, the laws of units and the Law of Right Human Relations. This is why we say that the family is sacred. The family must be united as much as possible. A group must be united. Nations must be united. Any treason against a nation is the greatest sin. Any treason against human unity is also the greatest sin because it is against that Will, that cosmic Wheel that grinds everything that opposes unity. Unity is formed only through the technique of right relations.

There is harmony of music and harmony of colors. There is harmony of movements. Those actions and events that are in disharmony within and with each other create sickness and disturbances. They create disturbances in the brain and the mind.

There are a few techniques that can be used to create right human relations:

*1. Create units.* I am referring to every aspect of life. The greatest honor of a human being is to adapt himself in such a way that he is an asset in a group. He is a source of inspiration who energizes others. He is a person who inspires others and leads them to their destiny by acting in such a way that their understanding is more and more clear and their visions are purer in their minds.

Each one is going to act as a source of inspiration, rather than a hindrance, in group life, in national and in international life. This is the ideal that politics must follow. From century to century, politics has been changing. Democracy, as an ideal, is an effort to adapt everyone's worth to the Supreme Purpose.

*2. Have a common service project.* You must have a magnet to magnetize the elements and create orchestration and stabilization, creativity, and sensitivity in people and lead them to the Purpose. In this case the magnet is a common service project. I do not say a self-interest project, a money making project, an increasing-your-ego project, a show-off project, a revenge project, or a hate project, but a service project, which means you are giving yourself to something greater than yourself.

You must have a service project to create right human relations in humanity. Musicians must compose their music; legislators must create laws; politicians must wisely use politics in such a way that they bring humanity to accept right human relationships. First you must have a service project, and then use your service to lead people to the ultimate Purpose, which is the revelation of Inner Divinity through right human relationship.

The Tibetan Master informs us that each nation has a motto.[1]

Everyone can create his own keynote, an individual service project to integrate his whole personality. When an athlete says that he wants to win a gold medal at the Olympics, to some degree he puts a project in front of himself. Because of that project, he eats well, he exercises well, he creates better emotional, mental, and spiritual equipment to meet the demands of that project. When you have a service project, everything within you slowly and naturally coordinates and cooperates with each other to make the unit, the man or woman, achieve the project.

From the simplest to the most complex project, it is the same process. You are going to have a service project. For example, the leader of a nation is going to gather his advisors and ask, "What role should we play in the world so that humanity achieves peace, harmony, and prosperity?"

Let us say that we have fifty people who are specialists in all aspects of a car meet and ask, "How can we make this car the perfect car?" One small group says, "We are specialists in wheels and steering." Another group specializes in the transmission, another the ignition, another the

1. Alice A. Bailey, *The Destiny of the Nations* (New York: Lucis Publishing Company, 1974), p. 50. That motto is a service project. The motto for the United States of America is, "I light the way." This is a national service project. Each citizen of the nation must really work to light the way, to create right human relations, to disperse darkness, and to create bridges between nations and super-human Beings.

brakes, etc. Everyone will do his utmost, without showing off, to make the best possible car to drive.

If any one of the members loses the vision of the perfect car, he works for his self-interest, and his self-interest works against the interest of the whole group that is creating a beautiful car. Those who are leaders in large companies and corporations know about this concept of orchestrating and synthesizing all of the elements working in that firm for a great project.

How nice it will be when fathers and mothers gather their children and say, "Let's create a service project for the community." The project itself and serving the project integrate the units. You will create integration in your group and in your society only when there is a project and only when you selflessly dedicate yourself to that project. A great scientist can create an airplane that flies for thousands of miles. But, to create a unit and a group requires more scientific knowledge than to create an airplane.

You are going to have projects for yourself individually, as well as work within the group. To dedicate yourself increasingly to those projects will create integration within you. Integration in a group comes only when there is a service project toward which everyone dedicates and sacrifices himself. By doing this, integration comes into being automatically and naturally. Integration is the flower of right relations.

In this integration process there are men and women of vanity, ego, "my interest," "your interest," "my revenge," "your revenge," hurt feelings, and past memories. With such orchestration, nothing great can be accomplished. You can put three people on a committee. Then listen to what they are discussing. "Didn't you tell me five years ago that I was stupid?" Forget such things. I sometimes put the most obnoxious people together in a committee so that they learn how to integrate with each other. Two of them can be sane while the third one is a real "monkey." The monkey will agitate the other two to death. The monkey teaches them how to control the monkey. Nature does this for you.

If, in all fields of human endeavor, leaders direct the interests of their people toward the unity of mankind and toward right human relations, in the year 2000, we — as one humanity — will be able to respond to the energy of the Most High and make a real breakthrough into the New Age.

# $Q_{\&A}$

**Question:** *New thoughts often emerge in a group. Are these necessarily right?*

**Answer:** New ideas, new visions, new thoughts, new propositions are excellent and can help enrich the group, but they must not be based on showing off, vanity, ego, self-interest, revenge, or slander.

**Question:** *In a way, it seems like in the group project one may stop one's own creativity and become almost like a robot.*

**Answer:** No! Higher, more advanced groups are formed by people who are free thinkers. Free thinking does not mean to oppose each other. Free thinking means to compliment each other.

Let us say that I am building a car. You say, "Let's make it a computerized car." If I say, "No," I am wrong because I am preventing the progress of the form. If new ideas and new plans come which promote the advancement, integration, and usefulness of the group in the future, they must be welcomed. We are not speaking about mechanicalness. We are referring to real creativity. But, of course, one needs to know also the mystery of right timing.

> **Question:** *If you have a new thought that is totally different from the vision of the group, would you have to leave your own group?*

**Answer:** Not necessarily. There are many techniques that can be used. For example, if you are presenting a formula of advanced astronomy to children, that would be stupid. You would not be adapting yourself to their level. This is why we say that cooperating on a group service project is a science.

Suppose there is a group that is in the process of maturing. It is not yet on a level where it can take advanced ideas and successfully work with them. That group must be taken very slowly through the ABC's until the members love and trust you and are able to assimilate your ideas. They must see that you are really sacrificial and are not taking the group in diverse directions. You must create ways to convince them to accept your propositions, your formulas, and your visions. When your ideas are assimilated, you will not have difficulty.

If a man comes to a group and presents a huge idea to a group that is not ready, everyone will feel discouraged and may leave the group. That man did not act wisely. One can even destroy a group with his high voltage ideas. First preparation, then the increase of voltage.

> **Question:** *Regarding the relationship between men and women, one purpose of the relationship is to grow. Another purpose is*

*to integrate oneself. Are these supposed to*
*occur at the same time?*

**Answer:** They should take place simultaneously. In the formation of units or groups, two things happen. First, all weaknesses and stupidities that exist in the members are drawn out. Second, the hidden potentials also within the members are drawn out. The group's survival, or the unit's survival, depends on which side of your nature is dominating. Are you drawing out the weaknesses and stupidities continuously, and not drawing out the possibilities and potentials of the group members? If you are drawing out and calling forth the potentials hidden within the people, that group will survive. But if you are continuously bringing the trash out of the group members, that group will disintegrate.

An important principle in the formation of groups or families is the principle of drawing out possibilities and potentials from the group members. For example, a wife says to her husband, "You have never taken me to Las Vegas." The man says, "You did this, this, and this." That family is not going to survive because they are emphasizing only unpleasant elements in their life.

Another way to build units is by gearing yourself into that Universal Law which builds units and integrates them. When you do this, you start drawing out the best things hidden in others. When beautiful qualities start coming out of yourself and others, the integration and the integrity of the family is guaranteed.

The same principle applies to a group. The group units come together with their magnetism, with their aura, and with other qualities and draw lots of "pus" or diamonds out of each other. The leadership must be very intelligent to see and balance these events and conditions.

It is good to draw out the pus, to a certain degree, but not at the expense of drawing out the good qualities in each other. When the percentage of these two is balanced, the group, on the one hand, cleans the pus and, on the other, brings out the goodness, beauty, and other qualities for the use of the group.

This is a science. You are consciously going to practice these things. When you meet opposition such as gossip, slander, etc., you automatically react. What would happen if you did not react? Instead of reacting, you could scientifically solve the problem.

This humanity is our big family. We must make every effort possible to direct the minds of people toward peace, harmony, freedom, one world, one humanity. Those who work for this project will be blessed in all coming ages.

Let people of the world realize that it is possible to live as one family, one world. Such a world will have all the potentials needed to come in contact with very advanced cultures existing in the Universe.

> **Question:** *Can you give some tips on ways to inspire the leader of an organization who has egocentricity?*

**Answer:** Such a leader can destroy the organization, but he will eventually learn.

Leadership is a serious science. In the future, people must not take leadership positions unless they are born for it or unless they are educated, trained, and can prove that they can be leaders.

Leadership means to be a nucleus or seed of a tree. If the seed or the nucleus is empty, or worm-like vices are eating it, you cannot expect a beautiful tree or a beautiful flower to come out. The seed of a group or a nation must be healthy. That seed is not necessarily an individual. It can be a group. An atom is composed of many elements. Likewise, a group can be formed of many people.

Future groups will be formed on the formula of the Universe. Our Universe is built on the formula of seven. In human understanding, those seven are manifested as

1. Politics

2. Education

3. Communication

4. Arts

5. Science

6. Religion

7. Economy

Any group that is truly forming must have these seven departments. Each of these departments has a corresponding ray, a specific quality. These seven departments must be built in the group by the persons who belong to these rays — to these characteristics. For example, you cannot put a politician into the field of economics. An artist does not fit well into the scientific field. Suppose a man is influenced primarily by the Seventh Ray. He can act as an economist or financier in the group. If you put the wrong person in such a position, the work will not be done well. Knowing the rays is a science. In the future, great leaders will know the rays of co-workers and place them in the right position.

The politicians in a group must be First Ray, and communicators must be Third Ray. If you are not putting people in the right position, the group can still go forward if there is devotion, dedication, and aspiration, but it can progress more quickly and more strongly when everyone is in the right position, just like the workings of a precision instrument. For example, a philosopher works on the Third Ray. You can put a Third Ray person in a leadership role, but he or she will talk and philosophize until people get sick of it. He is not strong in the area of politics and diplomacy, but he can work in the communication field.

Now, to come to your question. If a leader of a group is egocentric, the members may leave him, confront him, or ask a spiritual leader of another group to have a very close talk with him.

Of course, certain members, with their outstanding nobility, can inspire him and expand his consciousness, approaching him with real respect and appreciation. Sometimes we cannot see the real character of a leader and thus fabricate things about him. We may even see our own projections on him.

> **Question:** *What are the skills needed that will bring out the diamonds in the group and enable the group to stay in focus?*

**Answer:** In any group formation, for example in a family, the first duty is to cultivate a spirit of appreciation. This is lacking in most families at this time. Husbands do not appreciate their wives, and wives do not appreciate their husbands. Group members do not appreciate each other enough.

The second duty is, to search for beauty and potentials in each other. I remember a young woman who was failing in her life. I told her, "You are an artist. Did you know that?" "Am I?" She is now a great painter. I kept pulling out her inner potentials.

Sometimes husbands and wives are jealous of each other. This is common. You must be careful not to be jealous. When you are jealous, you hate to see beauty in others.

I also remember a woman who had a very beautiful dancer's body. She wanted to be a ballerina, but her husband said, "No. I don't want people looking at your body. I am jealous." He killed her talent. We must say, "You are a musician. You are a composer. You are an artist. I will support you," if they really are in our opinion. Sometimes we must sacrifice our own interests in order to support our husband, wife, children, or friends. If their talent is great and in the process of blooming, let it bloom. Don't stop it. Appreciate the beauty and potential of others. Create conditions in which they can exercise their talents.

**Question:** *Is respect different from appreciation?*

**Answer:** Most people "respect" others in order to bring them to the place where they can stab them in the back. Respect does not guarantee that you are "safe" in the hands of those who respect you. Respect does not mean that the man or woman who is respecting you also appreciates you. There is a subtle difference. Even the policeman respects you, but he still writes a ticket!

**Question:** *Is it better if a group member has the same general interest as the group, or if he has diversified interests?*

**Answer:** If the group members do not have a common interest, how can they stay together? But a common interest does not mean that they are created out of the same mold. They can have various talents, in various fields, and this makes the group richer. They can have different opinions on different subjects, but, above all, they must know how their thoughts affect the group consciousness, and they must have the commitment to work for the plan and goals of the group.

You are going to put yourself in conditions and situations in which your many potentials are challenged. For example, if I am a musician and totally dedicated to art, sometimes it is better to go to the field of science and see how I can fit there. In this way, things that are hidden in me, while I am in the field of art, come out through the field of science.

Each of us is a multisided diamond. It is not good to polish only one side; we must polish all sides. But, for the immediate need and for special requirements, we let a particular side of our nature be useful for the group work.

There are real advantages to a multidimensional concept. For example, a group of people are on their way to play in the orchestra. Suddenly on the way, the car stops. You demonstrate your mechanical talents at that moment and make the car run again. You do not need to play the violin to start the car.

I remember when five of us were traveling on horseback and entered a river. A leach stuck to the arm of one of the boys. He was trying to pull it off, but I said, "No, wait." I heated an iron and held it on the leach and it fell off. At such times, your interest is in the field where you are needed. You are going to expose facets of your diamond, the possibilities and talents that you have, and use them in the conditions where you have to meet a need.

Sometimes you say, "I am a violinist in an orchestra with two hundred other violinists. No one is applauding me. They are applauding the orchestra." In this case, your ego becomes activated. You may become part of a group where people adore you and flatter your ego, but this does not contribute to your spiritual progress. In group work, you have to work for the group. By working for the group, you follow the laws of the Universe.

**Question:** *What happens to the fragrance of the group as it blooms forth?*

**Answer:** Symbolically, the fragrance of the group is the influence and impressions that it gives to others. Once I visited an organization where two young women began telling me about their group. I said, "Wonderful. I would like to be a member of this group." I went inside and saw that ten or fifteen people were eating. They invited me to eat with them and I noticed that they were gossiping and slandering each other to such a degree that I said, "There is no fragrance here." Fragrance is the harmony, the influence, and the impressions that you give to others.

**Question:** *What should you do if you are part of a group that has lost its commitment to a vision?*

**Answer:** Don't stay there. You are wasting your time. But, be sure that your decision and your observations are not based on your vanities. I have seen many people say, "I am already a high degree initiate. I don't need this group." If you are really clear that your observation is not based on your vanity, ego, hurt feelings, jealousy, revengefulness, and old memories, you have graduated from that group and you should not stay there. Go to a higher group if your decision is pure. If not, try to transform the group with your beauty.

We are told that certain disciples, for two or three incarnations, sacrifice their progress to help members of a group to progress. Where is such sacrifice today? Most people say, "I am better than this group." Okay, leave it

and go to another group, but who is going to inspire them
and be an example of sacrifice for them if you are sure that
you are so great?

> **Question:** *If you are working in a corpora-
> tion and you are trying to establish trust,
> your goal being to open people to New Age
> type thinking, how do you do this?*

**Answer:** Don't think that corporate heads, other people with
degrees and diplomas, are always better. Often, on their
level, they are "children." First you must understand what
they are and how much they can expand. For example, a
balloon can expand only one foot. If you try to expand it
ten feet, it will burst. You must first understand the capacity
of those you are trying to help. Give them a little less than
enough so that they like you instead of hate you. If someone
speaks about concepts that you cannot understand or put
into practice, you will say, "What is he talking about?"
People change others because of their wisdom and high-
level beingness.

> **Question:** *When a person comes in contact
> with a group leader, he may have both
> positive and negative feelings toward the
> leader. How does one sift through this and
> really contact the true feelings and poten-
> tials?*

**Answer:** As far as the leader is concerned, he will not tell
you, "You are an ugly duckling. Everything is ugly in you.
Your mind is ugly, your face is ugly," etc. This would not
give him an opportunity to help. He can expose you, maybe,
to one percent of your ugliness and ninety percent of your
beauty. In this way, you can balance yourself. If you start

hating him, there is no hope for him to help. This is a science.

The group members must also emphasize more beauty in each other and maybe only one percent of the ugliness that is hurting the group. Even this one percent is sometimes better given through hints. The direct exposure of our weaknesses is very painful and creates reactions.

I once went with a man on a long journey. He was so beautiful. He had ninety percent good qualities. But he had one quality that was hurting me very much. I said to myself, "If you can stand this long journey of driving and flying for eighteen hours, you are a great man." I smiled, cooperated, and did not say anything about his irritating quality. At the end of the journey, I said to him, "You know, I am sometimes very stingy." He understood immediately. But I "bled" so that he could understand it. In this way, I didn't break our great friendship.

In order to contact your true feelings and potentials, you must learn to do these things. But you cannot learn them until you are exposed to group life and learn the techniques involved in group formation. Many people are so holy, sitting on a mountain top in a cave. They think that everyone must worship them. Work in a group, in a city, within the laws of that area, with this and that complication; then your true nature will appear. The group is a touch stone. It brings everything out in people. Even if people do not talk about your weaknesses, you can observe how ugly you are. The concept of the group is so important. The formation of groups is under a Universal Law, and we are just realizing it. You cannot stop this Law. It is better to understand that Law and the science of building a group life.

Families are formed, and families mean problems, whether we like it or not. We have many different groups, such as political groups, social groups, religious groups, business groups, etc. These groups are also full of head-aches. The greatest headache is to be a member of a group, but we cannot grow without that headache. Eventually, each group member will feel one with the group, and each group will prepare to feel one with a nation.

To feel like a nation means to have millions of levels of headaches. The time will come when each nation will feel one with humanity. Humanity will have to solve many problems. It is impossible to do otherwise. We are going to prepare ourselves to have the headache of being one human-ity. Imagine how many millions of dedicated people it will take to make the brotherhood of humanity a reality. We will do it because we have to obey that Cosmic Will. This is not a theory or a concept. It is reality. You are a unit. You have a body now. What can you do with it? It is best to keep that body healthy, happy, and prosperous. You have a family and a nation. There is going to be a united nations, the brotherhood of humanity. Eventually you are going to be a conscious part of the Galaxy.

A great Teacher says that the Entity that is ensouling the whole Solar System is taking an initiation. He is taking an initiation because every part of that body is helping Him reach that initiation. Consciously and unconsciously, every-one is helping. Every time you work for Beauty, Goodness, Truth, Freedom, and Joy, you are helping that Great Entity go forward a little further.

When your body, emotions, and mind are healthy, your soul is progressing. If they are unhealthy, you go downhill. You are going to study the science of how to make this planet healthy. Imagine that you are in a boat which has a hole where water is entering. There are ten people with you on the boat. One of the ten is shaving and trimming his beard. You call him and say, "Hey, there is a hole here. Come help us save this boat." But the man says, "The most important thing for me to do now is to shave and trim my beard." How stupid a man would be to say such a thing under those circumstances, but many human beings are just like that man. They say, "Who cares about the boat. My shaving and my beard are more important than the boat."

To repeat, the first technique in group formation is to cultivate the spirit of appreciation. The second technique is to search for beauty and potentials in each other.

The third technique is to subordinate your personal interests to the goal of achieving the service project. For example, you are preparing a drama. Maybe people in the drama do not like each other. Maybe they have various criticisms and feelings, but, no matter what, that drama must be performed. The players must subordinate their little wishes, little angers, desires, hatreds, jealousies, and slanders to the common project so that it manifests.

Once in our meeting hall, we built a bookroom. I gave the duty of painting it to four ladies. I told them that I did not care what color they chose, that it would be up to them. One month passed and the room was still not painted. Finally, I asked them why it was not painted. They said, "Do you want to know why?"

I said, "Yes."

They said, "One person wants green, one wants yellow, one wants blue, and one wants orange. We cannot agree on what color to paint it."

I said, "How silly. Just do it!"

They said, "We can't."

I said, "Just do it." The next day they all resigned. So I myself painted it an eggshell color.

When they saw it they said, "We didn't want that color."

I said, "Whether you like it or not, we have to have the room painted." The project must be completed. The show must go on. Why do we create such stupid disagreements? The ego prevents progress. Most of our disagreements are so ridiculous, and we do not see it. We must come to our senses.

Later, they asked me what my reason was in painting the room myself. I replied, "For one month, we'll have green, then one month blue, and so forth, so that everyone is satisfied." One of the ladies said, "What if I don't live three months, and my color did not appear?"

These ladies were interested in their individual likes and dislikes, forgetting about the completion of the project. It is good to give your ideas, but try to find a point of agreement. If you do not force your own likes and dislikes and see the common need, you may find points of agreement. One must negotiate with love and joy, but if you act as an ego, you lose the whole point of the game.

Sometimes in group activities, the leaders do not give a specific order but say, "Just do it." If people do absolutely wrong, the leaders whisper to them, "Why was this wrong?" It was wrong because it did not fit the project. They leave people free to do most anything they want, except to act against each other. Sometimes they allow even that, in order for the pus to come out.

The fourth technique is to look closely at yourself, and uproot your egotistic, self-seeking, self-interested, vain, and separative tendencies. Sometimes these tendencies come from other lives. You bring them with you in order to create problems. Sometimes it is good to create problems because you reveal many sides to your nature. You are not going to be afraid of seeing various faults in your nature.

Once we had a division in our organization. One group said, "We are going to stay in this hall on this land." The other group said, "We are going to sell this land and buy another piece of property." After listening for two hours to both groups, I said to each of them, "Present a statement saying why it is more economical, spiritual, etc. to stay, and why it is not economical, etc. to stay here." For seven months the two groups prepared their statements. When they came to the meeting, they had nothing substantial to report. They were really embarrassed. I told both groups I was disgusted with them and I disbanded them. They did not have any reason or logic for what they wanted to do. They were using the issue to satisfy their ego and to feel superior to each other.

Search for reason and logic to support your plans. If there is no substance behind what you want to do, why do it? Sometimes a self-seeking person will create a new section in a group so he can be the chairman of that section. A person who does not have the necessary technical knowledge, for example, wants to be in charge of the recording equipment.

We have many vanities and egos like this. Place them in their right position. There are millions of people who say they have many qualities that they do not have. They say they know things that they do not. Vanity is a pseudo image people have of themselves. When this condition exists in you, you cannot be yourself. And until you can be yourself, you cannot be successful in group work.

The fifth technique is to realize that the common project is a body in which you are an organ. Your success is to work for the body of the common project. If you cannot do this, do not stay and create hindrances. If you stay, then adjust, adapt, and transform yourself.

Let us say that a person is organizing a choir. Imagine what will happen if two people in the choir say, "I don't want to sing that."

"What do you want to sing?"

"I want to sing something else."

This attitude does not work. The common project demands that you sing a song in the best way possible. If you do not want to sing, it is better to say, "I am not well today, and I don't want to sing." This is acceptable. In addition, when everyone starts singing, do not sing so loudly that everyone notices your voice. When you do this, you are becoming a "goose." These things are simple and common.

The sixth technique is to be aware that there are six vipers that we continue to repeat, causing problems in right human relations.

**Fear** is the first viper. If you have any kind of fear in you from the group or from various other sources, you always translate the principles, the ideas, the projects, and the vision of the group through your fear. Once, while I was in the army, one of the boys had tremendous fear. If a mouse ran by, he would think that airplanes were about to drop bombs. One day some soldiers were sitting and eating in a cabin, and this boy shouted, "Get ready! They are coming! Hide behind the curtain!" Automatically the soldiers did as he said and opened fire and killed many of their friends.

Fear does not allow you to be reasonable, logical, factual, and realistic. Be careful in working with people who are in fear. They will mislead you. Do not follow fear. M.M. says that "fear is not a good guide." Fear is a very bad guide. The problem of fear can be solved logically, but it is the most obnoxious kind of flea that penetrates every side of your being. A person may have two hundred kinds of fear. There is fear of death, fear of accidents, fear of failure and defeat, fear of being ugly, etc. You can get rid of fear by concentrating your mind on that within you which is your Core, and say the following mantram:

*More radiant than the sun,*
*purer than the snow,*
*subtler than the ether*
*is the Self,*
*the Spirit within my heart.*
*I am that Self,*
*that Self am I.*

**Anger** is the second viper. It makes you impose and dominate, using your vanities, ego, etc. In a group, anger does not work. It does not work in any constructive project. You must adapt yourself to your position in the group and use it in the best way you can. This is the way groups should work.

"My decision, my plan," does not work in a group. There is a group plan. You may propose and present things. You may give great ideas and visions, but then you must detach from them.

Group work proceeds with those units who know how to detach themselves. Detachment is so important. If you have a great project and insist upon your own opinions and ideas without considering others, people will reject your project. But if you detach from your ego, they may look at it.

**Hate** is the third viper, the odor of separatism. It does not matter whether they are small or large hates. Hate simply does not work in groups. Hateful people must go through a psychological and psychoanalytical process to be healed. It is better to heal them before taking them into the group formation.

Hate contaminates a group or a nation. It contaminates humanity. Within nations there are certain groups that hate. They must be educated and cleaned.

**Jealousy** is the fourth viper. It does not work in groups. Right human relations are impossible when there is fear, anger, hate, or jealousy. A jealous person says of others, "Why do they have that? Why do they know those things? Why are they successful and shining? I must shine, not others."

Jealousy is a viper that must not be acceptable in groups. It brings devastation in the group life. Often jealous people are possessed by entities which make these people act in destructive ways. One can say that jealousy destroys friendship and prevents cooperation. Vanity, hate, and ego live on jealousy.

Never carry the viper of jealousy within your heart. When you become jealous of someone, immediately identify yourself with him or her, and the jealousy will slowly melt away. If a woman has the best car and you are jealous of her, be the woman in your imagination. Identify and fuse yourself with her. True identification melts jealousy away.

**Revenge**, the fifth viper, is also very bad. In a group and in a nation, right human relations cannot be created when there is desire for revenge. Revenge perpetuates events forever. "You kill me; I kill you. You kill me; I kill you." Such a psychology goes on forever. The history of humanity is the history of revenge and hatred.

**Slander** is the sixth viper. Slander is a very dangerous viper. There is personal and group slander. There is newspaper, radio, and television slander. Do not engage yourself in slander. It is karmically a very destructive thing to do to yourself. Always stand in the light and on the facts. Your intention must not be to destroy people. Your intention is to bring out the best that is hidden in them. You should do whatever is necessary to accomplish this.

Let us say that you need a mechanic, and a person applies who is not qualified. If you say to him, "You cannot do this job because you are not qualified for it," this is not slander. If you want to hire him, he must first go to school to get training. You are not going to take him as he is. He must change. But it would be slander if you said to everyone that this man was very corrupt and bad.

Slander is to belittle someone in the eyes of others. Slander also has a deeper meaning. If a person acts very silly, very stupidly and destructively, he is slandering the Divinity within himself. Let us say that you are a great man with a great family, and I am your son. Your reputation is very great. I drink and drug myself and fall into ugly conditions. In doing this, I am slandering my family. People must be very careful not to slander their group, themselves, their visions, and their projects.

People who are striving toward the vision of the year 2000 must not have any affinity with these six vipers.

Those who can conquer these vipers will become the shining lights on the path of humanity, and those who fall as slaves into the hands of these six vipers will slowly disintegrate physically, emotionally, mentally, and spiritually.

> **Question:** *How does one respond to a nation that is exhibiting all six of these vipers at one time?*

**Answer:** We must go to the roots of that nation's problems, but, first, we must not think that only one nation is doing such things. Maybe we are also doing such things. Maybe the most respected members of government are expressing these vipers.

When you read *Hiawatha*,[2] you will see the importance of forming an international confederation on the foundation of protecting the *purpose* of the confederation, not the

---

2. *Hiawatha and the Great Peace.*

members of the confederation. This ideal is not yet manifested because people do not yet see it. Because they do not see it, such a confederation did not manifest yet. Generally, nations are working against the rolling Wheel that is trying to bring all of humanity into synchronization and into being a symphony. We are acting against this Great Law. It is time now to make a new effort to understand these New Age principles.

Every nation makes positive contributions, and every nation creates many obstacles. We would be fools not to see what is going on. Sometimes evil things are done under the cover of honey and cake. The bottom may still be rotten.

# 3

———•———

# *The Angel*
# *and*
# *Right Human Relations*

Right human relations begin to manifest in our lives when we contact our Higher Self.

A Spark came from the Almighty Sun and reached the plane of matter. The Spark was programmed by the Great Mind of the Universe to bloom, to express, and to expand. Throughout millions and millions of ages, the Spark built a body, a physical existence, an "I." When you ask most people who they are, they say, referring to the body, "Don't you see? This is me." After centuries, the Spark built another "I" that became the emotional ego. Another two hundred incarnations later, it built the lower mind and became a separate self — a mental ego.

The ego is an artificial, separate self. If the Spark is identified with the mental plane, it feels like a separate being and identifies with its pseudo freedom. It feels that it can do anything it wants to do, and everything must work for its interest. This is the ego.

Later, it advances to the Higher Mind where it becomes a soul. To be a soul means, theoretically, to accept the unity and synthesis of everything. All of its thoughts, emotions, and activities are programmed in such a way that they do not serve the individual self; they serve the All-Self. This is the soul level.

Following the soul level, the Spark enters the Intuitional Plane. It then advances to the Atmic, Monadic, and Divine Planes. But for a long time it stays in the Spiritual Triad, which is formed by the mental, intuitional, and atmic permanent atoms.

When the human soul enters the Spiritual Triad, he or she is an Arhat. An Arhat has three great qualities — Light, Love, and Power — which are pure light or pure reasoning, pure love and compassion, and pure willpower. Willpower means that all of an Arhat's being resonates with the Will and Purpose of the Creator.

The Higher Self is our Guardian Angel. In psychology, It is referred to as the Transpersonal Self. It is also known as the Solar Angel, the Inner Watch, the Inner Guardian, the Inner Guide, or, as some religions believe, the Guardian Angel. In the womb of the Guardian Angel, the human soul takes form. As the man becomes in tune and totally integrated with the Solar Angel, he becomes a Soul-infused personality. In that degree and on that level, he becomes totally filled with goodwill and with the spirit of right human relations. This is why man must contact his Guardian Angel. As he contacts this Higher Self, he lives, he thinks, and he speaks within the framework of right human relations.

The Guardian Angel is all-inclusive and sacrificial. As the human being advances into the Guardian Angel's light and aura, he becomes all-inclusive, all-sacrificial, all-loving, all-compassionate, plus he develops pure intelligence and the awareness of the Hierarchy, and he demonstrates total harmlessness and a striving toward the future. This means that as one goes toward the Guardian Angel and fuses with It, his consciousness becomes one with the Higher Self, and he is filled with total harmlessness.

The Guardian Angel teaches us, impresses our mind, and inspires us to be a man or woman of goodwill and right human relations.

Those who contact the Guardian Angel show the following signs:

1. The first sign is an awakening of conscience. When we desire and strive to come in contact with the Solar Angel, our conscience develops within us. This is an indication that we are coming in contact with that Inner Guardian. We call this the development of the conscience. People have a conscience when they have contact with their Solar Angel. This can be a conscious or unconscious contact.

When people slowly withdraw from the Solar Angel, their conscience dies. They become brutal criminals, terrorists, murderers, etc. They fall into their ego and their physical, emotional, and mental traps.

We are going to observe our conscience. If we say something or if we think and do something that our conscience does not approve, we should not do it. If we ignore the conscience, we put ourselves into a very bad situation which creates karma and diminishes our energy, our intellect, and our creative power.

By observing the events and actions in your life, you will see how practical and realistic these concepts are. For example, if you are not obeying your conscience, you will see how complications gather on your path. To prevent this, do not do things that bother your conscience. In all religions, the conscience is highly respected. It is the guidance of the Solar Angel.

2. The second sign is the Inner Voice. The Inner Voice is higher than the conscience. When you develop your conscience, you will slowly start listening to the Real Voice that is talking within you. This is sometimes referred to as the "Voice of Silence." Many people have had the experience of "hearing" this Voice. When you want to go this or that way, sometimes the Voice will say to you, "Don't do that" or "Do this." This is direct communication with your Solar Angel. It is a very, very uplifting experience and also a fearsome experience if you do not obey that Voice.

3. The third sign is having a direct impression of what you must do, or visually seeing what the plan is for you.

These are three advanced signs of contact between you and your Solar Angel.

You can develop these three aspects by obeying your conscience. Do not do anything your conscience says is wrong to do. Everyone who does something wrong knows that it is wrong. If you know that some action, thought, or feeling is bothering you, do not express it, do not talk about it. If you feel that you did something by mistake, correct it. By so doing, you create a closer bridge and a closer communication with your Higher Self. Your Solar Angel sees everything and makes you feel that you are doing wrong, if you are. Some people do not need any advice from anyone because the Advisor, the Wise One, is in contact with them.

If you create sensitivity toward your Solar Angel, you will be right in everything because He will say what to do.

When you learn to obey your Inner Voice, your Inner Conscience, 80% of the time, the Solar Angel will suddenly disappear. You will feel lonely and that you have been left alone. That is the moment when you will be left alone to exercise your own potential.

The Solar Angel lets you go, to walk by yourself. Suppose you have a child and you say, "Hold my finger." Then you walk with him. You say to him, "Pay attention, that is the wall; that is the water; that is fire," etc. When he is no longer a child, you do not need to hold his hand. You let him learn his own lessons, but you still watch him.

In the same way, the Guardian Angel still watches you. He leaves you permanently at the moment of the Fourth Initiation. At the Fourth Initiation, it is certain that you are not going to backslide. There must be a guarantee that "this person is not going back to the mess of the old ways of living." In the next few incarnations following that, you prepare to be a Master.

The Solar Angel lives a double life. He is like a Great Teacher. He specializes in Higher University levels, but He also teaches various classes at lower levels. When the classes are over, He goes to His specialized work. The Solar Angel is not totally perfect. There is no end to perfection. Perfection is achieved level by level. As you advance, you become more and more perfect. The Solar Angel is also on the path of evolution. Wise Ones tell us that even God is striving toward perfection at His own level. There is nothing in the Universe that is not continuously striving toward perfection. This is the beauty of the Teaching. If there is a level where everything is perfect, you will ask, "Then what?" If there is nothing, you will be disappointed. God is the Infinite, ever-expanding One.

# $Q_{\&A}$

**Question:** *When a person lives in the lower mind and he thinks he can do anything he wants to do, does that have to play itself out?*

**Answer:** Things that are not good for your future can be bypassed through having a wise Teacher, great and holy literature, advice, and wisdom.

If you fall into darkness, you may remain in it for ten incarnations. People can get stuck in places that are not their right place. You can bypass these pitfalls. You can have a very brief experience with evil, then understand the whole issue and not dwell in it. For example, everyone knows what jealousy is and how it feels. Some people stay in it for ages, and others just know about it and discard it. If you can immediately pass through it, that is fine.

**Question:** *Can you tell us how to recognize the Voice of the Solar Angel versus other voices that might be trying to mislead us?*

**Answer:** Immediately when the Solar Angel starts giving advice, your vices, your old memories, or sneaky entities also express things to your mind to sidetrack you. But if you have a foundation, if you have learned to obey your conscience, such dangers are eliminated. You sense right from wrong. You know when you are doing something wrong, but you do it in spite of your conscience advising you not to. You say, "Shut up. I don't care about you."

Right human relations begin the moment we start having contact with our Higher Self. In the mantram, *"The sons of men are one and I am one with them,"* it should say

*"The souls of men are one...."* The Oversoul is the One. As we go higher into the Oversoul, the Higher Self, we become closer to each other.

It is just like climbing a mountain. You start at the bottom, a little far from each other. As you get closer to the top of the mountain, the people climbing the mountain form a circle.

As you get closer to your Guardian Angel, you become closer to each other and to humanity. This creates right human relations. As you get closer to the Solar Angel, you learn the science of how to adapt yourself and to orchestrate yourself with the steps of everyone climbing the mountain. You are going to notice that you, as a group, are one entity. That entity's feet cannot climb to the mountain top without using its hands, fingers, head, nose, eyes, etc.

You are going to have group consciousness, which means to think of all group members as yourself. If you have this group consciousness, you will walk together and encourage each other. When someone falls, you will heal and encourage him, eventually inspiring him to climb with you. If someone does not climb, one part of yourself is not climbing. You cannot climb successfully unless all of your parts climb together.

The Ageless Wisdom says that if you are not fitting into a group, it is better for you not to be a part of it. You can stop the group's progress, confuse the members, and create many difficulties for them. Or, you can inspire the group to strive together. Being a member of a group requires sacrifice, love, compassion, understanding, and especially self-abnegation — forgetting yourself in the interests of the group. This creates the science of right human relations.

**Question:** *What will happen in the year 2000 when there might be a separation between*

*those who are willing to accept right human
relations and those who will not?*

**Answer:** The energy that is going to hit will test everyone
and everything. If you are responding to that energy, your
entire creative system, you or your group, will start expanding and becoming more creative and alive. If you are
reacting to that energy, degeneration will set in — mentally,
emotionally, and physically.

I have been seeing these responses and reactions in
humanity since 1975.[1] Since that date, the number and
incidences of degenerative diseases have been increasing.
In the first chapter of *Symphony of the Zodiac*,[2] I wrote
about degenerative diseases increasing because of reactions
to the energies.

This incoming energy will split humanity into two
parts. If one of them is equipped with sophisticated weapons, war and destruction may occur. If the major percentage
of humanity is responding to the energies, they will try to
impress or sometimes impose their visions and inspirations
on the rest of humanity.

We might also see slow degeneration, as we are experiencing today. There are millions of tons of poisons and
various pollutants thrown into every aspect of life. Much of
this pollution we are experiencing today may have an effect
fifty years from now. Some scientists even think that two
hundred years from now, many women will not be able to
conceive because their genetic systems will be very distorted. The various types of X rays and other forms of
poisons entering into our bodies on a daily basis will
eventually create impotence in men and cause women to be

1. For clarification regarding response and reaction, please refer to *Cosmic Shocks.*
2. *Symphony of the Zodiac,* 2nd rev. ed.

unable to bear children. If we do not respond, "our goose is cooked." Humanity is now on that dangerous bridge. We are either going forward, or we are sinking.

When we use the term "disciples," we are not referring to followers of religions. We are speaking about those men and women with vision who understand the current situation. They have an influence on humanity as a result of disciplining their whole life. A disciple can be in business, in the legal profession, in religion, the arts, education, science, communication, or politics. If disciples increase in number, they will save this planet.

We are seeing many, many signs that people are awakening and even thinking that it is too late to save the planet from the ozone damage, from chemicals, insecticides, and various other poisons. People have started to panic.

It is a little late, but there is still a chance. The year 2000 will be the date when we are either going to degenerate or build an unimaginable future of beauty.

The world has enough science, enough philosophy, enough communication, enough of everything to make life on this planet a paradise, but we have not done this. We poison the oceans from which we get fish to eat. It was recently indicated that 80% of the fish in the world are polluted, and we are eating them. We will awaken because we have to obey that Cosmic Will. This is not a theory or a concept. It is reality.

The Tibetan Master urges disciples, until the year 2000, to make extraordinary efforts to shape themselves, their families, their groups, and their environment. *Regardless of what we have done in the past, in less than ten years we can change the world if we can change ourselves. Disciples are the foundation of the future new world.*

**Question:** *Does this apply to groups as well as individuals?*

**Answer:** This applies to groups, nations, and humanity.

**Question:** *Does this contact with higher realms occur every two thousand years?*

**Answer:** Everything is cyclic and rhythmic in the Universe. It is not always the same number of years. It changes according to the Universal Computer. Some people think that everything is set. It is not. Everything is set according to the purpose and level of things that have to change. Life is not static. It is an ever-changing, ever-adapting existence. Changes sometimes take two or three thousand years, and you would need two hundred incarnations to realize or to register them. When you take two steps, ten fleas die and two hundred fleas are born. If people had continuity of consciousness, they would see where the changes are coming from, where the rhythm is, where it is cut, bridged, and so forth.

Leadership is tied to right human relations, and leadership is tied to contact with your Inner Guardian. No one can be a right leader if he or she is not controlled, inspired, or directed by an inner vision and the Inner Voice that guides him or her.

Leadership begins with leading yourself. Ask, "Who am I to be leading myself?" You have a body, or a group, that is like a spoiled child. How can you guide it? Guide it on how to sit, how to rest, what to eat, what not to eat, how to have right human relations, how to exercise, how to dance, how to be happy, etc. You are going to lead your body. Once you start leading your body, you are in the first degree of leadership. If you are drinking and doping yourself, there is no leadership in you. Your body is dragging you.

It is very important to start leadership with your physical body. You may say to your body, "I want you to stand erect and beautiful. I want you to make good gestures. I want you to smile pleasantly and have control over your voice. I want you to have control over your stomach, your sex, your mouth, and speech. I want you to have control over your eyes," etc.

Next, you are going to control your emotional life, but control of your thoughts is the most difficult discipline. Do you sometimes worry? Do you suddenly awaken with fears and various other worries? Of course you do. How can you control thoughts such as defeat, excitement, thoughts of sex, of prestige, honor, degrees, reputation, things that are missed or are going to be missed? Can you have control over these things and say, "I don't want to hear any of this. I am going to rest"?

Leadership takes time. And when you start controlling, guiding, and orchestrating your thoughts according to what you want, you slowly become a greater and greater leader.

When we go to the foundation of leadership and ask, "What is leadership really?" we see that leadership is to put every "nut," every "piston," every "screw," and every "lever" in such a condition and situation that they do the right job for the entire machine. This creates right human relations.

This whole life is a conscious God. We are living and moving in Him. We are having our existence in Him. Every moment that Great, Conscious Life utilizes us according to what we are and according to where the need is. The only thing lacking in us is the realization, or consciousness, of how Great that Mind is.

When we start realizing that the Great Mind is utilizing us here and there, we will cooperate with Him and be a co-worker of that Great Existence instead of becoming a drag on Him.

You are in a place or in a group not necessarily because you wanted to be but because you reached a certain frequency and attracted certain people, and certain people were attracted to you in order to continue the movement of building units. This is why you must not betray each other, no matter where you are.

In the *Bhagavad Gita*, it says, "Wherever *dharma* puts you, stay there and work." There is only one work. Anyone who is doing anything is actually working for the construction of the same vision, usually without knowing about it. For example, the carpenters, the electricians, the plumbers, etc. are each doing one important aspect of the construction. If you consider each of their labors separately, it appears to be nonsense, but when you synthesize their labors, you see the whole purpose of the construction.

The various groups throughout the world are now doing their respective work on the "temple." There are builders. There are destroyers. There are children. For example, we build at night. Then, in the early morning we see that half of our work is destroyed. We build again. This whole process is going on continuously — building and destroying. Builders sometimes do not know why they are building and what they are doing, but the Teacher comes and says, "Put some cement here." "Okay, we will." They may not know what that cement will do in the future, but the Super Engineer knows that this and that wall and this and that little labor will build the parts of the great building.

You each have your responsibility, your *dharma*. Your *dharma* is the exact location, the exact job, the exact position that you should be in. It is given to you, and you are going to work there. For example, the exact locations are given to the cells in your body. The brain cells are different from the bone and hair cells. Each category of cell has seventy-seven thousand jobs to do in your body, but not one of the cells is fighting against the other cells to take over another's duty. If this does occur, you become ill. Brain cells are professors and specialize in brain function. The eye cells are the most advanced cells in the human body. The eye is the mirror of the Soul. If a fingernail cell suddenly says, "I am going to operate like a cell in the brain," you will have a problem.

You are already orchestrated by the Highest Computer in the Universe to be wherever you are. In devotion, wherever you are, make it perfect. You are building the parts of the Cosmic Temple.

The Oversoul gives a chance to you, on various levels, to have certain new positions. But you can spoil, mislead, become blind and deaf to the Inner Sounds. Then you find yourself in the wrong location and in the wrong job. The Oversoul did not do that; you did it. In another phase, as you come closer to your Solar Angel, and if you are not already in your correct location, you will go to it. This is a matter of becoming closer to your Higher Self in order to find yourself, your location, and the people with whom you are going to offer a great labor. They are attracted to you. Actually, you are attracted to each other for a specific labor.

> **Question:** *Since all of us are part of this greater Existence, do the forces that oppose the evolution of humanity exist by permission of this Greater Existence?*

**Answer:** Of course. They have permission to exist. They can be part of the same Plan. Their function depends on how they are being utilized by you! Fire is an energy which can be used constructively or destructively. Who is going to be blamed when the fire destroys something? You, as the operator, will be blamed. But you are eventually given experience, knowledge, and the science of how to use that energy. There is nothing in the whole Universe that cannot be used for the greatest good of humanity. But you are going to learn the techniques in order to utilize them. The prophet Mohammed told a story in a lecture. He said, "There was a man called Noah. He built his ark, but he didn't know how to make his ark go north, south, east, or west. It was left to the chance of the winds. One day, he observed that the ark was traveling north, and it turned to go exactly west. He said, 'What is happening? There is something wrong.' After searching and searching, he went to the back of the ark and noticed that a small Satan had a little piece of wood in his hand and was affecting the direction of the ark. Noah said, 'Ahh, I learned something here.' From that knowledge came the discovery of the rudder."

The prophet Mohammed told this story to illustrate that if one is intelligent enough, he can learn great lessons from the opposition. Actually, the greatest teachers are our enemies. M.M. says, "Bless your enemies because they are your free teachers. They advertise about you and your work better than your friends."

**Question:** *Do the Initiates use the invisible forces to carry their carriage to the top of the mountain?*

**Answer:** Yes, they do. For example, there was a story about a bishop living in Armenia. He was the head of a large temple. There were two hundred students who became more and more lazy while living in the monastery and did less and less work. In one of the buildings, there was a huge fireplace which was very dirty because no one was removing the ashes. One day the bishop ordered two entities to clean away the ashes.

Behind such stories, there is some reality. If you have control of yourself and of a situation, you can use even obnoxious people to reach your goal. I did something like this in the school where I was the principal. One of the students was obnoxious. He would bully and beat everyone. After a while, I managed to be his friend. I took him to restaurants, to the beach, etc. Eventually, he liked and trusted me. Finally, I said to him, "You are going to be the officer in charge of student control in the school." He was the right boy for that job.

M.M., in another very beautiful expression, says, "All winds serve to turn our windmill." Regardless from what direction the wind comes, you use it to grind your flour. You must have a keen intellect to do this because it is a very dangerous game.

Another example is that we sometimes use certain poisons in small amounts for medicinal and healing purposes. Many germs and viruses are killed with these poisons. It is possible to use the dark forces, if you know how to do it.

> **Question:** *If God is the Supreme Origin of everything, where do dark forces come from originally?*

**Answer:** I have written about this in *The Science of Meditation.*[3] Dark forces are not a creation of God. People mislead themselves and believe that dark forces are created by God.

---

3. *The Science of Meditation*, Chapter 28.

Do not worry about dark forces being in heaven. Dark forces are all around you. They are in the form of criminals, war mongers, exploiters, etc.

# 4

—•—

# Contact With the Higher Self

There are fifteen steps that prepare us to make contact with the Higher Self through right human relations, group consciousness, and cooperation. These steps are as follows:

1. *Obedience to higher principles creates right human relations.* Obedience improves your willpower. You demonstrate more endurance, patience, strength, stability, courage, and daring as you come closer to your Solar Angel, your Inner Guardian. You can use these qualities in your communities, in your social relationships, and in your leadership. There is no leadership without these qualities.

2. *Recognition of the rights of other people and their worth.* It is very important to develop the quality of seeing the value in others, to appreciate them and to respect them. If a group exercises these qualities, you will see improvement in the group. Respect each other's rights. Of course,

you must develop a finer consciousness in order to see the
rights of others. We are referring to the rights of their
existence, their freedom, their joy, and their pleasures. If
you do not respect the rights of others, your rights will be
taken from you.

This concept also works in politics. In the future,
politicians will be those who respect the rights of others. In
the United Nations there is a "Bill of Human Rights," but
how many of us are honoring it? It is massacred daily. When
the new disciples assume high positions, they will respect
human rights from A to Z. People will no longer be able to
say, for example, that Black people have no rights because
they are black. This respect of others' rights, appreciation,
and recognition comes when you become closer to your
Solar Angel. Otherwise, you do not have these qualities.
**The year 2000 must be proclaimed as the year of the
recognition of human rights.**

3. *Recognition of the Divine Presence living in others.*
No matter what people are, there is a Divine Presence in
them. Your duty is to call forth that Divine Presence by
becoming a midwife to bring forth that Child that is their
Essence, their contact with the Higher Self.

4. *Getting closer to your Higher Self.* This causes you
to take natural steps to challenge people to demonstrate and
manifest the potentials latent in them. You inspire and
encourage them. You always present a challenge for them,
the challenge of dancing, singing, composing, and the
challenge of leadership. You try to bring the potentials out
of them so that you increase, your group increases, and
humanity increases in value.

Each of you is a large, locked treasury. There is so
much beauty, talent, and potential in you. Who is going to

unlock them? If you are jealous or afraid, you cannot do this. If you are hating, you cannot do it. If you are slanderous and revengeful, you cannot do it. But if you can unlock this treasury, it means you are closer to your Solar Angel, and you want to see beauty in everyone and an increasing beauty in the world.

People who think in an old-fashioned way say, "We must be rich, and they must be poor. We must use them as our donkeys." That age is over. In the New Age, people will think, "The more people become wealthy and prosperous, the more I will enjoy my life." It is not good to enjoy life when everyone around you is sick and poor. Still, we have millions of individuals and organizations that work to make others poor and themselves wealthy. It just does not work in the long run. It destroys humanity.

5. *A person who comes closer to his Higher Self protects others*, even if it means endangering his own life. He also protects people from themselves. He protects them from enemies. He protects them from ignorance. He protects them from inner confusion. He protects them from falling into hatred, fear, revenge, greed, and self-deception.

As you get closer to your Guardian Angel, your eyes open wide. You have a big eye, and you are able to protect people.

When I was a student in a monastery, there was a boy who protected everyone who was in trouble. Suppose you stomped on my foot and hurt me, and I started to beat you. This boy would come and protect you.

I asked one of the teachers what kind of psychology this was. The teacher replied, "That boy is a masterpiece. He protects everyone because he feels no one should be beaten or abused. It is a natural sense for him to protect people."

Do you protect each other? When someone gossips or slanders another, do you protect the person who is being slandered? Or do you say, "Yes, I know. She is very bad." You may awaken suddenly and say, "I am going to protect those who are under attack, whether they are right or wrong." This is another way of protection.

6. *A person who is taking a stand with his Solar Angel is very careful and discriminating about what he hears and sees.* He is able to see the truth and the facts instead of the games that hide the truth.

Some people read the newspaper as if it were the word of absolute truth. Know that it is paid politics. You must develop a state of mind which does not believe wholesale things that people tell you. Stop being an automaton. Use your intellect and your intuition to see what is going on.

If someone tells you that the dollar is falling, maybe he is lying in order to sell you gold. There are many games like that. For example, nations fabricate stories against each other because they hate each other. People may start hating a particular nation because so many articles are written against it. Stop and think. Think for yourself, and see what is your conclusion. We are fooled and deceived with a continuous barrage of propaganda.

7. *You serve and sacrifice for others and become an example for others.* When you start learning right human relations and get closer to your Solar Angel, you slowly become a leader, which means that through your frequency, influence, and impression, you lead people to themselves.

The first duty of a leader is to lead others to their Inner Self, to contact with their Solar Angel. Unless you do this, you cannot lead them. They cannot understand what you are talking about. A true, advanced group is formed by those who have had at least a few contacts with their Solar Angel.

If you meet resistance from people, it means that you were not intelligent enough to approach people properly and give the right lessons to them. Your "hook" was not professional. If one cannot win someone, he must sit and say, "What did I do wrong?"

Maybe you are talking about algebra and that person has no concept of algebra. Teach him the ABC's and make him your friend. Sometimes it is better not to teach anything to anyone until he becomes your friend. He must trust you. Teaching is a science. It is not just telling people, "We are the only way to fly; come and join us." That does not work.

8. *Doing **only** your own duty and responsibility.*

9. *Encouraging others to do their own duties.* In *The Bhagavad Gita*, Krishna says, "Do only your own duty and don't engage yourself in doing the duty of others." We learn this from our body. The eye does not function as the toes. The nose does not work as a tongue. They are all assigned to their duties. If they start mixing their duties, man would be lost. Sometimes in groups the "nose" starts doing the work of the "head," and the "head" starts doing the work of the "toes." Everything becomes distorted and confused. You must put every person in his or her right place. The leadership must be very intelligent to do this.

In group formation, the leader must be very strict and put everyone in the right place. If people are not in their right places, they can be real "headaches," and others cannot easily clean these "headaches." One of the jobs of a leader is to put people in the right place. The leader is also going to be in his or her right place. If the leader is not in the right place, everyone will be in the wrong place.

10. *Exercise control upon past, unpleasant memories.* If you are a group member, you are no longer going to remind yourself and other members of what happened in the past. It is difficult to build a new group consciousness by referring to past memories. The past is past. Let it go. Of course, you must be careful that the past is not repeated. But by always having past failures and mistakes in your mind, you are spoiling and poisoning the present situation, and you are not seeing the issues that are presented to you in a clear light.

11. *Develop the joy of cooperation.* Sometimes there are people around you who say something just to contradict you. If you say, "This is right," they say, "No, that is wrong." If you say, "This is good," they immediately say, "That is bad." This is a habit that has roots in a form of showing off, an inferiority or a superiority complex.

The leader must also be careful not to repeat this sort of behavior. He must develop a sense of cooperation. Even if the leader knows that what others are saying is totally wrong, he can wait for a few minutes and see the motives. Why are they doing this, or why are they saying that? Then he can give a slight hint to suggest otherwise, so that he will not be trapped if he is wrong.

Let us say that you go home from a meeting feeling very defeated and like a failure because there were arguments and hurt feelings expressed. You do not sleep that night. The next day you go to work and cannot look at the faces of those with whom you argued the day before. You sit and think, "Wouldn't it have been better if I had cooperated? Why was I doing that?" Something must be built so that we cooperate with each other.

Cooperation saves your energy and time. Try to understand the joy of cooperation. You must have this experience and immediately record it the moment you feel the joy of cooperation — mental and emotional cooperation, cooperative action, all kinds of cooperation. Immediately record how happy you were when you cooperated. The joy of cooperation will lead you into higher understanding in the future.[1]

12. *Try to be a conscious part of a group unit.* Ask, "Is this my duty?" Do your duty perfectly, and know why you are doing that duty and for what reasons. Do your part consciously, not mechanically. Try to do your conscious part for the benefit of the group, not for the benefit of yourself.

13. *Be obedient to your Higher Self.*

14. *Be obedient to your Teacher, who is introduced to you by your Higher Self.* Once you find your Teacher, he or she cooperates with your Solar Angel and makes you ready to be not only a part of a group created on the objective level but also a part of an Ashram that functions in Higher Planes.

15. *To have better contact with your Solar Angel, you must act as an observer*, observing all that your mind, your emotions, and your body are doing. The better you observe, the closer you get to your Solar Angel.

In the Teaching of the Buddha, consciousness is symbolically explained as belonging to ten worlds. Wherever your consciousness is, you are in that world. People did not

---

1. Please refer to *The Psychology of Cooperation and Group Consciousness.*

understand this concept at first. They thought that Buddha was referring to ten locations on this globe. Later when He gave advanced Teachings, He explained that these ten worlds exist in our consciousness.

The first "land" of consciousness is called *hell*. This state of consciousness is called hell because of continuous suffering. We sometimes have a state of consciousness that bothers us day and night when we are guilty of doing wrong, are planning to do something obnoxious, or when we are disobeying our Higher Self. In this state, we are living in the hell part of our consciousness.

*Hunger* is the second state. There is a part of our consciousness that is symbolized by hunger. This refers to hunger for food, hunger for sex, to eat and eat and eat; there is always a hunger that cannot be satisfied. Such a person is like a hungry dog. Even if such a person received your respect, he wants more respect. If he is praised, he wants more praise.

*Animality* or *bestiality* is the third state. People sometimes act like beasts by "eating and devouring" each other for their own self-interests. They destroy the reputation of individuals, groups, and nations to satisfy their own bestiality. They cannot let others enjoy life. They are bestial in their behavior, in their emotions, thoughts, and planning. This bestial behavior runs against right human relations.

The fourth state of consciousness is *anger*. Anger is another state of consciousness where you want to impose yourself on others, no matter what. "I told you to do that!" Anger is forceful imposition of your position or your self-interests, glamors, illusions, lies, ambitions, and exploitations. We can see this throughout the history of humanity. Most wars and conflicts were sparked by a person or a group who was in anger. It has been a point of infection that has led so many to war. But historians are careful to put a sweet coating on that infection so that we do not see that conflict starts from anger, hunger, animality, and hell.

Next is the state of *humanliness*. An animal does not care if it lives at the expense of others. Humanliness is when you cause others to live at your expense. Christ gave this principle in a very abstract symbol when He said, "I am the bread of life; eat it." He did not say, "You are the bread of life with nice butter on it; let me eat you!"

The sixth state is *heavenliness*. According to the Teaching, heavenliness has two octaves. There are people who are always happy, no matter what happens. We sometimes call this state "ignorant happiness," insensitiveness, or indifference to human needs, pain, and suffering. Buddha was not referring to this lower state. In the higher part, the disciple is really in heaven, in the higher mental plane, where he contemplates all beauties, all future achievements of humanity. He feels extremely happy, which is real joy.

The next state of consciousness is *learning*. A part of your consciousness always wants to learn new things. Learning is the result of your experiences. Eventually your learning becomes realization. Realization is a result of knowing where and how you can use the things that you have learned.

The next state is *realization*. In this state, you know what you can do with your knowledge, but still there is a little self-interest lurking behind your actions.

The ninth state is that state of consciousness which we call *discipleship*. Discipleship is totally different from the previous eight states of consciousness. Discipleship is **"Whatever I have or have had, whatever I know, whatever I can do is dedicated to the service of humanity, consciously offered."** If you live a life of discipleship for two or three lives, you will reach the tenth state of consciousness.

The tenth is the state of *Christhood* or *Buddhahood*. This is the perfection that one reaches in consciousness in one cycle. After that cycle, you will break that state, becoming greater and more illuminated.

You can use the above information to see where you stand on the ladder of your evolution.

# 5

—•—

## *Self-Transformation*

There is a great urge in every human being, whether
or not he is conscious of it. This is the urge toward
perfection. A person can have one percent, fifty percent, or
one-hundred percent of this urge. If anyone wants to
improve physically, emotionally, and mentally in his business or in his health, there is the urge available to be more
beautiful, more advanced, more progressed, and more
spiritually uplifted. This urge eventually comes to the stage
where it turns into the urge for self-transformation. Self-
transformation starts the moment a person feels this urge
and consciously wants to do something with himself.

What does transformation mean? Transformation
means to change an existing form or renew and regenerate
it. We have various forms that must be subjected to transformation. The first form is our physical body. The second
and third forms are our emotional and mental bodies. The
forms of our emotions, our thoughts, and the forms we are

expressing as actions, feelings, and thoughts must be transformed.

To transform means to change, improve, and regenerate something. In every human being, there is the urge to progress and transform. There is this programming in every soul, and this programming causes the individual to strive toward that unknown programming which is not really revealed in his consciousness, but it is there. You feel it is there. All of your striving, all of your improvements and transformations are responses to this programming.

Transformation is not easy. It is a very difficult process. For centuries you have built your bodies in certain patterns. Certain habits of your physical body, certain manifestations of your emotional and mental natures are crystallized to such a degree that, when you decide to change them, you meet tremendous opposition. It is sometimes embarrassing. You want to do something great, but you cannot. You want to be holy, but you become "poly." You want to complete something perfectly, but you mess it up or create disorder. You do this because the forms that you built throughout centuries attack the forces of change within you. They do not want to be bothered. The mind says, "I want to slander, to gossip." The emotions say, "I want to be afraid, to be angry." You have great difficulty dealing with this spoiled child that is yourself. It is embarrassing not only for you, but for others as well. It is especially embarrassing for those who see the games you are playing with yourself.

One of these games is when you imitate that you are changed. You imitate that you are really good and that you are transformed. This is the worst thing you can do because it builds another layer of hypocrisy in your character. The second, third, and fourth layers are more difficult to crush and destroy, or to cut through, than the first.

Transformation is a very difficult process, but, once you feel the inner urge, you are going to make it. You are going to transform your life. This is what the urge is. From that moment forward, you take steps very scientifically and professionally to fight against your former self-image.

The forms that we have at the present are not ideal. For example, our body is not ideal. We are fat, we are thin; we are not perfectly proportioned; our body is slightly deformed and not really stable and healthy. It is not really radiant. Our emotional body is not ideal because most of us do not yet have developed astral bodies. And most people's mental body is in an embryonic stage. People think that if they know a few things in scientific or historical terms, they are cultivated and have a mature mental body, but this is not the case. Today, millions of tapes are available to put into the computer of our mind and help us pretend that we are something. This is another self-deception.

Ideal bodies have seven characteristics. If you want to build the ideal physical, emotional, mental, and higher bodies, and if they are in the ideal, progressing stage of development (there is always development), you must demonstrate seven characteristics:

1. *Beauty* is the first characteristic. First, you become beautiful mentally, then emotionally and physically.

Inner beauty manifests slowly and makes you a very attractive, handsome, or pretty manifestation. Your words and motives are really beautiful. Beauty, here, means great harmony and goal-fitness.

2. *Health* is the second characteristic. You not only look healthy, but you are healthy. You are healthy physically, emotionally, and mentally.

You sometimes manifest different stages of development. Physically you are forty-five years old, emotionally you are a baby, and mentally you are a savage. But, because people see your forty-five year old body, they say, "This is a man. This is a woman." They do not know that a young child and a savage are dwelling in you, nor that you are identified with these images.

You can easily see this in yourself and others. For example, this man is a professor, but emotionally he is a baby, and mentally he is "square." You can also see people in your environment whose three bodies are harmoniously developed. This is what health is.

A healthy person is one who has the same age in his three bodies. In the future, psychologists and psychiatrists will create sophisticated instruments to observe a person's physical, emotional, and mental age. There are an immeasurable number of mentally retarded people in the world, but the urge for transformation is still there, and all people, on their own level, are striving to be something and somebody. In this way, they will eventually meet that ideal archetype that is projected into their Self.

3. *Increasing sensitivity* is the third characteristic. When the physical, emotional and mental bodies, the emotions, and the thoughts are healthy and developing and are in the process of transformation, you see that the bodies are becoming physically, emotionally, and mentally very sensitive. Sometimes this sensitivity cycle drives you crazy because you register everything that is occurring around you physically, emotionally, and mentally. How can you balance yourself when this happens? Stability is to go through these storms without losing your foothold.

4. *The registration of developing senses* is the fourth characteristic. We say that we can see through our eyes, but an advanced artist is not seeing as we see. An artist's eyes are totally different from most people's. If an artist's eyes are 80% progressed, he or she is a genius. Some people do not hear certain things. They do not even discriminate in what they are hearing. Their ears are not developed. Their other physical senses are also not developed.

There are also emotional and mental senses. How can we see that these emotional and mental senses are developing? On the way toward transformation, our physical, emotional, mental, and higher senses start unfolding and developing and making us a central point of registration and control. The more information we have from the outer and inner worlds, the more control we have upon our mechanism. The greater control we have on our mechanism, the better we can use the information we are receiving from the outer and inner worlds. An average man sees the ocean, a tree, or a flower and says, "That is beautiful." But a man who has developed his senses sees a Cosmic Beauty and translates it into a work of art.

5. *Tuning in with the higher bodies* is the fifth characteristic. Transformation brings your physical body to a stage of development in which it slowly tunes in with the astral body. Then the astral body tunes in with the mental body. These three bodies coordinate and integrate with each other in the process of transformation. Not only with your physical body but also with your emotions, with your mind, and with your spirit, you are going to be a shining beauty in the world. That is the goal.

6. *Tuning in with the higher centers* is the sixth characteristic. As transformation proceeds within us, our radio

station starts receiving higher and higher sources of information.

One day a Great Teacher was asked, "How can you know so many things and answer any question asked?" He replied, "I tune in with the centers that are the authorities on these subjects." Evolving and developing senses eventually bring us into contact with higher centers of creativity, information, and knowledge. This is another goal toward which we are striving. We are not going to be gophers. We are going to graduate and eventually become human beings.

This is the process that we must have in our consciousness. We must observe where we are, what kinds of breakthroughs and conflicts we need, so that we can eventually destroy layers and layers of hindrances that we have accumulated around ourselves. All of us are involved in this transformation process.

*7. The creative process* is the seventh characteristic. When the physical, emotional, and mental bodies are healthy and the person has lofty thoughts, something wonderful appears. People become creative. They become creative in ideas, in emotions, in projects, etc., and they have a regenerative influence upon others. The healthy body regenerates other bodies and stimulates creativity in them. One who has a healthy body aligns himself with the higher centers and higher planes, and regenerates and develops his senses. He increases his sensitivity and becomes very healthy and beautiful.

Transformation induces change. There are two kinds of changes. One is transformation; the other is degeneration. In one, you are making changes that improve yourself based on your own archetype. In the other, you are making changes that cause your bodies to degenerate, atrophy, and eventually disappear.

If you sincerely want to transform yourself, you are going to pay the price for it. Through great labor, great intentions and perseverance, you are going to work very hard on yourself. This will prevent your bodies from degenerating.

How can you transform your bodies?

1. You cannot change your physical body by concentrating your whole attention on your physical body. No matter what you do to your physical body, you cannot transform it. You can eat right, sleep right, etc., but you cannot change it. This is the fallacy of the new health developments. You can change your body by changing your habits and cultivating higher virtues. Habits are patterns built into your etheric body. Your etheric body controls your health and the form of your body. Habits must be changed if you want to change your body. Drop a habit and you will see the changes that occur in your physical body.

2. You cannot change your emotional nature unless you change your emotional habits and cultivate higher virtues. When you change your emotions, your emotional body changes. Exercising your emotional body with astral gymnastics, etc. does not help. You must change your emotional attitudes and relationships with others. If the emotions do not change, your emotional body degenerates.

In a sense, the transformation process is a cleansing process of your habits and the mechanical nature that you have developed throughout the ages. To sublimate and transform your emotional body, you need to change the patterns and forms of your emotions. When the emotional forms and crystallized patterns are changed, you will feel a tremendous beauty in your emotions. You do not need to work directly on your emotional body.

3. You cannot transform your mental body unless you transform your thinking habits and cultivate higher virtues. There was a very beautiful and healthy young man who was always failing his university studies. I asked myself, "What is wrong with this boy?" When I discovered the problem, we immediately started to change his thinking habits. His thinking was going through a pattern that was learned from others and imposed upon him. His mind immediately opened after a few exercises, and he graduated from the university with high honors. Through such experiences, I have seen that you cannot work directly on the bodies. You must cultivate higher virtues.

What is the "Self" in Self-transformation? The Self is your individuality, the human soul. The Self is your real, Inner Core which carries within Itself the archetype that is given to you by the Great Consciousness of Nature. Each seed has an inner seed containing the archetypes. This is the Self. The Self is the One Who orchestrates all of your movements, all of your physical, emotional, and mental actions. Eventually It develops them to such a degree that you are in direct contact with It.

One may ask what the role of the Solar Angel is. The Solar Angel is the bridge or contact between the personality and the Self. The personality is the deluded human soul. He is not yet aware of his Self-hood. Most of the time, the Self is asleep in the personality. It is not even in existence.

As the human soul begins to awaken, he acts as the owner of the personality. The Solar Angel tries to make the human soul aware of his Self-hood. For a long time, the Solar Angel acts for the Self. It is at the Third Initiation that the human soul sees glimpses of his Self-hood, and the True Self begins to emerge in cooperation with the Solar Angel. The human soul continues to awaken until the Fourth Initiation, when the Solar Angel leaves the person, and the human soul, as the Driver, takes the reins of the carriage in his own hands.

The Solar Angel, from the time of individualization to the Fourth Initiation, tries to awaken man into his divinity or Self-hood.

Once the human soul comes into being, it becomes a central cause for transformation on higher planes, in higher worlds, and a cause in relation to the world of men.

To clarify this concept, the word "human soul" refers to your awareness unit, who controls your life — your physical body, your emotional body, and your mental body.

Self-transformation has seven stages:

1. Your body-self introduces changes in your life.

2. Your emotional-body-self controls your life.

3. Your mental-body-self controls your life and your environment.[1]

4. Your Teacher supervises and guides you.

5. Your Solar Angel inspires you to a better life.

6. You, as the human soul, control your own life.

---

1. These three selves are the organized elementals.

7. You, as the Self, control your whole mechanism
   and life.

The concept and phenomena of the Self begin with your
individualization, continue through your evolution, and
eventually you awaken into your true identity. Your Self-
hood "is a point of light within a greater Light."

In most cases, the Self is sleeping within. No matter
how awake you think you are, if you were really awake,
you would see how asleep you were.

How can the Self cause transformation if you do not
have a Self? This was a great mystery that was solved ages
and ages ago by Sages. They said, "You must have a
representative of your Self, and that is your Teacher. Your
Teacher will act as your Self, and if you obey your Self
one-hundred percent, you will obey your Teacher because
the Teacher is your Self."

Ancients thought that the best Teacher was the most
difficult Teacher. Such a Teacher makes your misery, hate,
and revenge come out so that eventually you come to a
moment when you are ready to break your "shells," your
limitations.

The most difficult duty of the Teacher is to deal with
obnoxious people. They react. They pounce and bite. They
do not know what the Teacher is doing.

The Teacher is taking a chisel and hammer and making
a beautiful statue from a rock. Of course the rock — your
physical, emotional, and mental elementals — will scream
with each blow of the chisel, "What are you doing? You
are violating my freedom, my beauty, my genius, my
experiences." But, the elementals do not know what is going
on. If you react to the Teacher, you may lose your life or
there may be no possibility that you can be an awakened
human being. If you respond to him, it is possible that you

will have a chance to improve. But he will tell you that every step to improve you and release you from that prison of your arrogance, your hatred, your treason, and your malice is a painful process for your Teacher. This is his duty. He makes you clean the waste and sewage so that you learn what you have created in the past.

The real Teacher makes you uncomfortable. Whenever you find that a Teacher is making you feel uncomfortable, it is the first sign that he is a Teacher. But be very careful of false, abusive, so-called "teachers" whose only aim is their own personal satisfaction, glorification, and financial and personal gain. Or, if a person is praising you and tolerating your stupid, sneaky actions, he is not a Teacher. He is exploiting you. Exploitation means to be a friend of people's obnoxiousness and personalities and never care for their spiritual awakening.

The Teacher acts as the representative of your Solar Angel, and then of your Self, until your Self awakens to such a degree that you can take over. You say to the Teacher, "I can do it now." He looks at you and if you are real, he says, "Do it for yourself now."

The first thing the Teacher wants you to do is to face your own stupidities. Unless you face your stupidities and shortcomings, you will not awaken to the state of consciousness you could have. The Teacher makes you angry. He makes you uncomfortable. You do not know what to do. If you turn this way, you are wrong. If you turn that way, you are wrong. When this happens, is the Teacher wrong? Is he playing with you? He is not. He is slowly, slowly focusing your mind until you see exactly what you are without deceiving yourself. The Teacher is a great help in the transformation process until your Self takes over.

There are many steps of transformation. For example:

1. Confrontation is the first step. Never try to hide from yourself or from your Teacher. At any moment that you are playing "hide and seek," you are ruining yourself. Confront yourself exactly as you are. Try not to hide your failures and your mistakes. Say, "Yes, I did it."

2. Never justify yourself. Christ never justified Himself, even in the "court."

3. Go to your Teacher and ask for the discipline you need, but not necessarily the discipline you expect. The discipline you need is the one you least expect.

You must go to your Teacher and ask, "What discipline do I need?" He may say, "Obey my suggestions even if they do not please you." Otherwise, stop being his student. If you stop seeing him and start slandering, cursing, and gossiping about him, you are burying yourself. But if you can face what he says and ask, "What is the plan behind his actions?" you are on the path of transformation.

4. Never use treason against your Higher Self and your Teacher — never. The greatest sin is acting against the Teacher. The Teacher can be a teacher on any level. There is only one stream of Light.

5. Always develop harmlessness and gratitude within your soul. Develop them in all situations and occasions without exception. If life kicks you, thank God for it. You are going to exercise harmlessness. If you can do this, you have begun to be a superhuman being.

Develop harmlessness and gratitude because these are two protective agents — giants really — that protect you from falling into slander, malice, and treason.

6. Be a fearless fighter to increase Light, to increase Beauty, to increase Goodness, Righteousness, Joy, and Freedom, and do not obey anyone unless your conscience tells you to do so.

With these six steps, you can really transform yourself. A real group must be built upon these principles. Many groups are not even aware of the existence of these principles. In fact, if they read about them, they will be against these principles.

When you start observing these principles, your trash will come to the surface, and you will have a "wonderful" time dealing with it.

# *Q&A*

**Question:** *When Christ saw Mary Magdalene, He did not make her face her trash.*

**Answer:** Really? Christ put the most intense and subtle pressure on her by showing His beauty. You can "kill" a man by showing your beauty, by showing your supreme joy, the attitude of your consciousness, and the depth you have. You do not need to tell people that they are naughty. Sometimes it is not necessary to come into direct contact with the trash of people. You are going to show directly your beauty, and if people are ready, they will awaken. Mary Magdalene became a very advanced disciple because of Christ's beauty. Of course, every beauty also attracts treason and ugliness.

**Question:** *Can you speak more on the development of sensitivity of the bodies?*

**Answer:** There are bodies that are not sensitive. On the other hand, there are people who touch your hand and know what you are feeling and thinking. This kind of communication reveals what you are. Your voice, your glances, and your aura reveal certain things. Sensitivity is like a very sensitive microphone that receives impressions in a 360 degree radius. But you must have the stability to stand undamaged at the fulcrum of this reception.

**Question:** *What is the distinction between being sensitive and being touchy?*

**Answer:** Sensitivity is the registration of impressions. Touchiness is the reaction of your personal, selfish intentions to exciting news, information, or impressions.

**Question:** *If a person was doing something and other people misjudged that person's reasons or goals, the person tries to explain or justify himself. If that person cannot make himself understood, then is it all lost?*

**Answer:** You are not going to justify yourself to your True Self or to your Teacher. You can try to make yourself clear to anyone else, if it helps. Sometimes, the more you justify, the more you are caught in their trap. We are looking at things from 360 degrees.

**Question:** *Are you saying that even when a whole group of people was disagreeing with Him, Christ did not justify Himself?*

**Answer:** He did not. This is why the prophet Isaiah says that "He went to the cross as a lamb for slaughter" to make contemporaries and future generations see the spirit of His sacrifice and victory. Because of His supreme sacrifice, everyone starts anew to feel the urge to perfection. This is why millions of churches and martyrs came into being. They were shaken into awakeness.

**Question:** *In order for a person to transform and change himself, must the discipline and knowledge of discipline come from the Teacher?*

**Answer:** Yes. Until he can be the Self.

**Question:** *Can the Teacher do this at a distance?*

**Answer:** Yes, the Teacher can exercise pressure by his thoughts, if the disciple accepts it. A good Teacher is not allowed to exercise pressure without acceptance from the student or disciple. It is much better when the Teacher is in close contact and sees the daily life of the student or disciple. Gurdjieff used many methods to reveal the hidden nature within his disciples. He was one of the most advanced Teachers. When the Teacher dies and your Self is not awake yet, the Teaching is lost. But if you are awake, you continue to walk in the Teaching.

It is difficult to have a hard Teacher. To have a hard Teacher means that the Teacher is going to have very, very strong nerves.

**Question:** *Where can you find such Teachers?*

**Answer:** If you are ready, the Teacher is everywhere. We are referring to real Teachers who are dedicated to their job. Of course, your friends, your children, even your enemies can also be nice teachers. When I pass through failures and shocking experiences, the next day my consciousness develops by many degrees.

You are going to learn everything — great experiences and great wisdom — from everyone. But you are going to be hard and tough enough to still cherish someone who slanders you. You see a person gossiping, slandering, and using malice toward you. Still, you want to know how you can save his life. You must make yourself available to dangers.

There are many Teachers who will "appear" if you are ready and worthy of it. If, by chance, you find one, do not lose him! When you are a real disciple, life is your Teacher. Holy Scriptures are your Teachers. Those who live according to the principles of the Holy Scriptures are your Teachers. If you have ears to listen, all of nature will talk to you and tell you how to live your life. After the year 2000, the respect toward the real Teachers will increase because many advanced Teachers will appear and make you feel the urgency to strive toward perfection under Their eyes.

After you meet a real Teacher, you notice a great change in your life. Your whole worshipped structure may shatter. You may make a sincere effort to improve — you will see great changes in yourself, even if you are tempted to hate your Teacher.

# 6

—•—

## *Toward Perfection*

What is striving? Some people work day and night to collect money and possessions. This is a very nice thing... because we need money and possessions. Others want to know and know and know. This is also good... because we need knowledge. There are also people who want to enjoy life. This is wonderful... because we need to enjoy life. But havingness, knowingness, and enjoying life do not change or transform us. If we add one more thing to these three, we will see that man is living a complete and beautiful life. The fourth element is beingness. This is a very important element to make us fulfill our life purpose.

Beingness means that we are going to change our physical, emotional, and mental natures. We want to live another step higher and transcend our nature. Nature created us, and we are now human beings. Can we be more than this?

Knowingness alone cannot lead you into the next step. Havingness and enjoyment alone cannot lead you to the next step of your evolution. But beingness, which is based on the transformation of your nature, leads you to other, higher states of consciousness and actualization.

Some people read and read and read. Others listen and listen. Some people collect many books in their library, and others have encyclopedic brains. But if you observe their lives, you will see that they are very poor. They do not have that inner glow, that inner experience of being something more than an ordinary human.

We have the idea impressed in our mind that we are human beings and that is all — there is nothing beyond this. This image can be destroyed only through striving.

I had a friend who one day said, "This is the life." Then one day he had an experience. He heard his Teacher's voice, and his Teacher was fifty miles away. The Teacher said, "Turn back immediately and walk to that village." He looked around, but he could not see Him. He had a profound experience there. Later, he wrote to his Teacher and said, "You spoke to me, and it was at the right time. You gave direction to me, and I saved a human being." This experience urged and inspired him to be something more than he was. *Striving is to be something more than you are.*

Another friend told me, "I was sleeping, and in my sleep I went to a lecture. The lecture was held on a mountain. A very tall human being was talking about politics. He warned, 'That city and that city and that city will be burned and destroyed. Immediately vacate these cities.' I woke up and said, 'What is happening? Is this true or false?' It was true. It happened exactly as He said." Another friend said, "I had an experience that showed me that it is possible to be out of your body and attend classes and gatherings and come in contact with Minds Who know more that you know.

They can see two, three, or fifty years into the future." All these stories challenged me and made me say, "I am going to be more than I am now."

We had a Teacher once who was seven feet tall. There was a girl who had a large bump growing on her wrist which disturbed her a great deal. She went to the doctors who suggested that it be surgically removed. I said to her, "Wait until the Teacher comes and see what He says." The Teacher came and, looking at her wrist, said to her, "Give me your hand." He held her hand and said, "It is gone." The bump had disappeared.

I have gathered from these experiences that there is something in human beings which, if cultivated, makes them more than what they are. I started searching for these things, going from one school to another, from one monastery to another, beginning at an early age. Finally, I found a Teacher who said, "You don't need regular studies. I will give you one huge book. You are going to study and learn from it day and night."

I said, "Give me that book. In what language is it written?"

"Oh, it is written in your language." I was very excited. He invited me to his office where he handed me a folded piece of paper and said, "This is your book."

I said, "This is my book?"

"Yes, this is your book. Open it."

I opened the paper and it said, "Continuously strive if you want to transcend yourself, and read the Book of Life."

From that time until today, I have been thinking about what striving is. I have written many articles, chapters, and books about striving, but his is the simplest explanation I know. Only through striving can you step out of what you are now.

You might ask, "Is it necessary to be something better than I am now?" If you do not become better than what you are now, you will not have health, joy, prosperity, success, and efficiency, and you will become worse.

Every minute, you are challenged. You are challenged in business, in health, in society, in the courts — everywhere! Life demands and forces you to strive. Only through striving can you enjoy life, have more, know more, and be more. The builders of the New Age are those who are perfecting themselves in the art of striving.

Striving is to cause your physical, emotional, and mental bodies slowly to refine, change their chemistry, and develop greater senses that can register more than they were registering before. These senses can transmit things to the world, to humanity, and to Space that you cannot imagine.

What will the physical body be like if you strive? First, observe the habits of your body. For example, a striving person will slowly develop control over his habits. It is easy to read a book and understand what it says, but it is not easy to drop a habit. A habit is an image in which you are crystallized. As long as you are living in that habit, you are like a snake that cannot shed its skin. You cannot grow out of the size that you are. To grow, you must destroy your mechanical habits — drinking habits, sex habits, sleeping habits, smoking habits, drug habits, eating habits, etc. You must be free of habits. Habits are just like clouds around your body which prevent energy circulation between your body and Space. Habits are crystallizations in your aura. Any energy that is coming to your body is translated through the forms of your habits as that energy is penetrating into your body. Eighty percent of the energy or impressions coming from Space is swallowed up by your habits. This is why you are weak and do not have energy. This is why you cannot grow spiritually. These habits are floating all around you and sapping you. They are like different entities.

What happens when you strive? The Ageless Wisdom says that our three vehicles — physical, emotional, and mental — have three qualities. One of the qualities is inertia. Most of our bodies — most everyone's bodies — have inertia. The second quality, which is a little more advanced, is motion or excitement. The third quality is rhythm, harmony, or radiation. Our cells have these three qualities. When our bodies are formed of cells which are ninety-percent inertia and ten percent motion, rhythm is not even present. This is a coarse body. Striving decreases the coarseness, the inertia, and the excitement, and brings rhythm, harmony, and radiation into our bodies.

There was a boy who would at times show signs of obsession and possession. I told the parents to take one of the boy's shirts or a jacket to the Teacher for His blessing, then to let the boy wear the clothing. They did this, and as long as he wore the clothing blessed by the Teacher, he never showed signs of obsession or possession.

What created this power, this psychic energy, in the Teacher? His body was dynamic. The energy that was latent in the atoms of his vehicles was released like atomic energy. His whole body was rhythmic. The energy, the radiation that he had, permeated his clothing. It was charged with psychic energy. Possessing entities, or obsessing thoughts or glamors, could not stand the power of his energy. This is the result of striving. Slowly, slowly we conquer our habits, and if we conquer one or two habits in ten years, we advance three hundred years.

The worldly "life" teaches us the exact opposite. Life says, "Eat, drink, and enjoy. Be mechanical." Mechanically you eat; mechanically you have sex; mechanically you drink; and mechanically you sleep. You cannot break this mechanicalness. Striving is an effort to break these mechanical patterns and change the chemistry, the substance, the principles of your body.

What does hatred do? It consumes the calcium from your bones and destroys your brain and liver. Very soon, medical doctors will be able to tell you this. Jealousy kills the hemoglobin in your blood and damages your spleen. Fear destroys your heart, poisons your blood, and eats your bones. Irritation creates poisons which spread throughout your nervous system. If you do not want these vipers, you must strive. Isn't striving beautiful and necessary? Of course! Striving is the "only way to fly." We are flying toward greatness, beauty, goodness, joy, and freedom.

Striving does not stop with the physical body. It goes to your emotional nature. Through striving you can transform your emotional nature.

A young man once said to me, "I found a very beautiful girlfriend, but I can't live with her."

"Why is that?" I asked.

"She is so jealous that I can't even say hello to my friends." Jealousy destroys you and your relationships. Jealousy prevents cooperation. Jealousy even destroys the creative talents that you have. Striving wipes away and cleans these things from your emotional nature, making it very magnetic and beautiful. Through striving, you will make your emotional nature full of peace, radiation, joy, freedom, and compassion. If you have these virtues, you will live for eighty or ninety years, or longer, because you are not in the hands of certain psychological "leeches" which can eat your psychic energy, your blood, and your soul. These vipers can destroy you.

Your emotional body has the capacity to transcend itself. Start exercising less fear, less anger, less hatred, less jealousy, less revenge, less gossip, and more control over your mouth. Can you do this? This is the Teaching. The Teaching is not knowing things. The Teaching is given to work on your beingness.

In the mental body, striving is to discipline our mental nature and free our mind from all of the various limitations we have built around our mind. We must make our mind an instrument of Light.

There are a few things in our mental plane that must be destroyed. One of them is vanity. In all great religions and traditions, vanity is an obnoxious vice. Vanity can be destroyed by striving.

The Teaching urges us to strive. In this kind of Teaching, there is no doctrine, no dogma, no "ism." This Teaching is not against anyone or anything. It is a Teaching that challenges you to surpass yourself.

Sometimes we think that we know everything. When we think that we know everything, we are in vanity. As a great philosopher once said, "I know one thing; I know that I don't know anything."

The more I learn, the less I know. The more I become, the more I strive to be a little better than before. Suppose I am now developed spiritually to a certain degree. From that level, I see that I have five hundred years of growth ahead. But, if I grow a little more, I will see that I have five million years to grow. Vanity is a mental block. We must destroy that vanity. When we are able to destroy that vanity, we come to our senses.

When I say to people, "You are not yet yourself. Please be yourself," they think and think. Then they say, "That is nonsense. I am myself. I am talking with you." You are not talking with me. Your posthypnotic suggestions are talking with me. Others are talking through you, and you think you are talking with me. If you can observe and catch yourself doing this, you will be so surprised. Sometimes you speak, sometimes you feel, and sometimes you do things that you never wanted to think, speak, feel, or do. Why is that?

Most of us have many masks on our faces. We present ourselves as other than what we really are. If you are presenting yourself as something different from what you are in reality, you are deceiving yourself into believing that you are something, that you know something, that you have something, and that you can do something. If these are not true, you are your own enemy by continuously deceiving yourself as well as others. Actually, we would never deceive each other if we would learn not to deceive ourselves. Striving is to clean that vanity.

We also have a big monster within ourselves called "ego." This ego is touchy, nosy, hypersensitive, and it can be hurt immediately. It reacts automatically. It cries and screams and creates a mess everywhere. This is our ego. We think that we are the center of the universe, and everyone must bow down and serve us. We pretend we are something that we are not.

Psychologically, the ego is identification with your false selves. Whenever you imagine yourself to be something other than what you are, you create a false image about you. When these false images increase, your "goose is cooked." You will try to catch up with and touch yourself, but you will not be able to. Many millions of people experience this. They ask, "Who am I?" How accurate is your answer? Who are you? Which one of the many masks are you? Today you are a king or queen. Tomorrow you will be something else. For the next hundred days, you will be a hundred different people. Which one are you really?

One day I went to one of my Teachers and said, "This man promised me something."

He asked, "Which man?"

I replied, "That man."

"But which man?"

"The one who has grey hair."

"My gosh," he said. "Listen, which man?"

I thought, "This Teacher is crazy. Let me not argue with him." I went swimming and what he said was going around in my mind, "Which man?" This question went on for one month in my mind, and finally I realized that when the man talked with me about something, he was lying. "Oh," I said, "this is the lying one, the deceiving one, the happy and sad one, the slandering one, the fearful one. Which side of the man was I referring to?"

Later, my Teacher said, "If that man were one person, his promise would be good, but if there are many men in one body, do not believe his promises because there is no one there permanently who can make a promise to you."

Don't you change your mind and your emotions many times daily? Don't you change your relationships many times? Who is doing that changing? Why is this? If you promised, why are you not fulfilling your promise? Actually, you did not promise. Something else was promising. But if you become united within yourself, if you become together and find your Real Self, people will believe that you will fulfill your promise.

Striving creates simplicity. Simplicity means to be yourself. Complication means to be millions of faces and characters. Simplicity is to say, to express, and to be exactly as you are.

There is also separatism. "I am better than others." "We are higher than they." "We are advanced and they are backward." "We are this color and this religion, and they are that color and that religion." This separatism is turning our planet into a planet of pain, sorrow, and suffering. This evil is in our mind. Striving means to conquer that evil!

Can you conquer separatism? Can you live for one day without thinking in terms of separatism? Try it! This is beingness. You may know many encyclopedias inside and out, but never have beingness.

Bank tellers receive millions of dollars, but when their paycheck comes, it is for far less. What about the millions that go through their hands? It does not belong to them. The books that you have read do not belong to you. The things that you have heard do not belong to you. What belongs to you? Only your own transformation is you. No one can take it from you. When you are a loving, pure, simple, sincere, giving, and sacrificing person, a person who is enlightened, no one can take from you what you are.

People and Nature can take anything from you that you are not. You are going to lose everything that you are not. You are going to lose your money and your land because you are not land and money. You will eventually lose all of your property because you are not your property. You are even going to lose your body because you are not the body. Only your True Self will remain. Things that do not belong to you will be taken away. If you are a smart business person, you will have things that no one can take from you. This is transformation. This is your beauty, your spiritual evolution, your transformation, and your transfiguration.

How can you strive if you are totally involved with your physical mess, if you are totally involved with your emotional hang-ups and turmoils? If your mind is blocked with vanity, ego, separatism, fanaticism, and illusions, how can you strive?

Your striving starts when you go to your Teacher and your Teacher says, "Don't smoke." Your Teacher will give the first lessons of striving. He will say, "Sit and learn meditation. Read this book, analyze it, assimilate and practice it." Your Teacher will be the source of inspiration to you. To cause you to strive, he or she will say, "Dress better than you do now. Make your hair better than it is now. Improve your make-up. Be faithful, trustworthy, and sincere. Develop virtues and become sacrificial. Be inclusive." Your Teacher will give you standards and challenge you to build these standards within you.

When you reach a certain level of "awakening," you will take your own destiny into your hands and start striving. In this second level, striving will change. You will challenge your body to be as beautiful as you dream it to be. The challenge starts to act within you. You do not have to have a Teacher. You are your own teacher. You will say to your emotions, "I don't like this hatred anymore. I do not like this jealousy, separatism, ego, vanity, and laziness. I don't want them." You start exercising greater and greater pressure upon your bodies so that the standards for your bodies are elevated. As you raise the standards for your bodies, your own standard rises. At this point, you begin entering into higher dimensions of consciousness.

# $Q_{\&A}$

**Question:** *There are times when you are striving to overcome habits. What does one do to overcome the frustration that occurs while striving?*

**Answer:** Overcome frustration by being like a child. When your father says don't eat a certain food, you do not eat it. Likewise, you must obey your Teacher. Nowadays, obedience is often translated as slavery. But obedience, in great monasteries and esoteric schools, is a great honor. If the

Teacher says, "Walk straight," regardless of how much you do not like to walk straight, you walk straight — because the Teacher said to do it. The Teacher is your guide until you are your own guide. This is the first lesson that you must learn.

The Teacher says, "You are going to bed at nine o'clock." But you do not go to bed at nine o'clock, so you do not have a Teacher. Because you do not have a Teacher, you are not a student, no matter how great your knowledge, no matter how many things you know. To have a Teacher means to obey him until you are your own teacher. Because you are not yet able to be your own teacher, you are going to obey your Teacher. The Teacher is five thousand years ahead of you. The Teacher can give you techniques on how to do these things. *Obedience is sensitivity to the demands of your Soul which are presented by your Teacher.* Nowadays, people obey their medical doctor as if he were a god. They obey because they think they will have good health. But they hate to obey their spiritual Teacher who is interested in making them healthy emotionally, mentally, and spiritually.

One day my Teacher told one of his financially successful friends, "I told you a hundred times not to fall into anger."

He answered, "I don't want to be your slave."

"But you obey every single word of your stockbroker," said the Teacher.

"Because," he answered, "I see the result of his words."

The Teacher did not talk any more. A few years later, the friend, in a moment of anger, killed his wife and himself.

We are told that in the pyramids there was an initiation ceremony for the Initiates who were going to take the Third Initiation — the Transfiguration. The Teacher would order each student, "Walk straight. Don't stop." The student would walk toward a wall, then stop and say, "This is a wall. How am I going to continue?" The Teacher would say, "Walk!" When the student failed to continue walking, the Teacher would touch the wall and it would immediately open. Inside, Great Ones would be waiting to initiate the student. The student did not obey the Teacher when He said, "Walk."

Obedience, in many so-called civilized countries, is synonymous with slavery. The Teacher comes and meets you only once in your life. If you do not lose that opportunity, you have it. If the Teacher says, "Don't do that," don't do it! "But I like it." There is no, "I like it. I want it." There is only one thing. You are going to obey him or her if you want to break your own limitations. You are not yet in a position to be your own boss. It is just like having a baby in your arms. The baby says, "I don't want this. I don't want that." You discipline him and say, "Do what I say." This is one method, one step you can use if you have the sensitivity to obey.

Sometimes I am very sorry that I did not always obey my Teacher. One day my Teacher said, "You are going to a village, but before you reach there, the road forks. Take the road to the right."

When we reached the fork, my horse wanted to turn right, but I said, "Did you also hear the Teacher? Now, listen to me. We will take the left road." I was almost killed on that road. I had to take drastic measures to save my life. Obey the Teacher!

> **Question:** *How do you recognize when you are being the false self?*

**Answer:** You always recognize it! You always see it, but you pretend that you do not! There are several signs that indicate you are being the false self. The first sign is that people no longer like you. People lie to you. They hate you. They are jealous of you. There is something wrong. Wrong things that exist within you attract wrong things from others. You see your image in the mirrors of others. Your image is what you hate in others. When you start hating something in others, it is yourself that you are hating. You are hating yourself in them. When this happens, you have a chance to see it. "Wow. I am hating myself. There must be something in me that I don't like. Because I don't like it, let me drop it." You must clearly observe yourself.

People think that if they read that book or listen to that lecture, they will graduate from the university. Then they will suddenly grow wings and be an angel. This is a hallucination. We have learned to take a pill for everything and be "cured."

In the spiritual life, there are no pills. You are going to sweat; you are going to fall and be humiliated. You will come to a state of consciousness where you will really hate yourself. Until you come to that stage, you are in self-delusion. A stage will come where you will say, "I don't like myself anymore." When you humble yourself, your Teacher will approach you.

We read in a wise man's book, "Humility is the sign of greatness. Glory follows humility." Humility means to throw out your false selves and start meeting your True Self. People ask why it is considered a good sign when people feel humble, or even lose hope for themselves. The answer is that when one no longer worships himself, it means he has now a higher vision, a higher standard in his heart, in comparison to which he feels short.

**Question:** *What is the best approach to break bad habits?*

**Answer:** The best thing is self-observation. When you are walking, when you are doing things, feeling things, reacting and responding to things, and when you are thinking, talking, writing, etc., observe yourself. Really, what are you doing, and why are you doing these things? This is the supreme method to cause you to meet, to recognize, and to know your Self. When you do something stupid, say, "This was really stupid. Why did I do that?"

But for one or two years, for example, never criticize yourself, even if you see that you were the most horrible person. Just observe it. Slowly, slowly clean yourself. No one can make you advance spiritually. You must make yourself advance by hearing and obeying Great Teachers. You have Great Teachers in all religions.

> **Question:** *If you are striving, is it true that you increase the abundance of joy in your life?*

**Answer:** At first, this does not happen. This is a warning for you. When you start cleaning your house, you immediately see how messy you are. All of the dirt, the mice, the scorpions, and the foxes come to the surface. You say, "My gosh. I didn't know that I was so bad." This is the test. If you overcome that test, the sunrise starts in your life. You must clean yourself, your subconscious, in order to be clean in the future.

We have billions and billions of registered diskettes or tapes in our subconscious mind. Most of these recordings are negative, obnoxious, and destructive. How can we clean them?

As you start developing spiritually, a certain amount of this mess comes to the surface. If you are lucky, you will not immediately release the whole sewage because you cannot handle it. Your Teacher will tell you how to face and clean it slowly. Often, the best method is meditation. Meditation burns away the past, subconscious trash naturally, without causing it to flood the surface of your consciousness. Even one of Christ's disciples confessed, "Lord, when I want to be beautiful, I am so ugly. I don't know what to do. I am so miserable." Because of the radiation of Jesus, all of the disciple's past trash was coming to the surface.

**Question:** *Why do we have an emotional body?*

**Answer:** If we did not have an emotional body, we would have a very difficult time relating to each other. If the emotional body is sublimated, it is the transmitter of the Intuitional Light. In the book of Revelation, something was stated that most people have not understood. "From now on, there will be no ocean, no water. There will be only a crystal mirror." The emotional body turns into a mirror that reflects the Divine Mysteries, the Divine Beauty.

**Question:** *Is striving an expression of our Divinity?*

**Answer:** Striving is not an expression of your Divinity because an "expression" can be real or false. Striving is the manifestation of your Inner Divinity. For example, the sun is shining and slowly destroying the fog, clouds, and mist so that eventually you can see the clear sky. This is what true striving is. Your sun must shine.

It is better to have a loving family, a beautiful environment, in which you have the most favorable conditions to bloom — just like a seedling. If you do not have these conditions, it is because you violated certain laws of Nature in the past, so Nature threw you into certain difficult situations so that you eventually get the green light.

The Creator of the Universe is waiting for us to come back Home. That magnetic pull is so strong that no one can say, "I don't have a chance." We are already in the magnetic field. God help us so that we stand in that magnetic field and go back to our Home. Where is the Home? Think about it!

As the year 2000 is approaching, we have to make ourselves ready to respond creatively to the energy which is going to be released. Those who will be able to respond to that energy will be the engineers of the New Era and of the new life.

# 7

———•———

## Striving


"... *the construction of one's own orbit depends upon striving.*"[1]

Striving builds the future Path on which you will travel.

If your striving is continuous, your orbit will expand and rise.

Your orbit is the field in which you live, the path on which you travel, the limit beyond which your actions stop, and the wall which protects your rights.

An advancing soul has a spiral orbit.

His orbits are on many planes simultaneously.

Striving nourishes all these spirals, keeping them sensitive and progressive.

The orbit determines the field of contact of the human soul.

---

1. Agni Yoga Society, *Infinity*, vol. 2 (New York: Agni Yoga Society, 1957), para. 435.

The human soul, through its magnetic power, produces the substance of the orbit. Each of our vehicles, like a spiral, has its orbit around the human soul.

The striving of the soul produces the energies, or the electromagnetic field, for the formation of the orbit.

Every ring of the orbit is the measure of control of the elements found in the field between the human soul and the orbit.

Striving determines the paths of orbits for each body and harmonizes each body's speed on each path.

Thus, by providing an orbit for each body, the human soul, through his striving, builds a magnetic field which turns into a communication network with the Universe.

One of the responsibilities of the human soul is to build his orbits in such a way that they do not violate the rights of the orbits of other souls, but instead cooperate with them.

Such a cooperation creates further opportunities for the human soul to expand his own orbits.

Solar Systems are created when many spiral orbits cooperate with each other and form a collective body for a greater purpose and for a greater labor.

Each system must have its Sun, the soul, that acts as the central Core for the system.

The striving of the soul determines the relationship and duties of each spiral to the Central Sun.

Cosmos is built by the power of striving. The power of striving is an effort to reveal and activate the initial archetypes in each Core and orchestrate the orbits according to It.

Creativity proceeds through the urge to form orbits, and through not only expanding the orbits but also through creating a life within the orbits in harmony with the speed of the orbits.

When the life within the orbits and the speed of the orbits synchronize, then the possibility is given to the orbits to expand, and the opportunity is given to the life in the orbits to transcend its labor of creativity.

When astronomers observe the stars and galaxies, they see the mechanics of these bodies, as if these heavenly bodies were machines abandoned in space. The astronomers do not think about the consciousness within these bodies which originates all that they see.

Each heavenly body, single or compound, lives through the power of striving. When striving is exhausted, the disintegration of orbits and systems begins. The Central Life — the Consciousness — withdraws and becomes a path of a Greater System.

In space, individual existence is only possible by striving to serve the Purpose of a collective Existence.

But on earth, this Law is not yet observed by human beings, though the human consciousness is becoming more sensitive to it.

Striving is a radioactive effort to reveal the Purpose concealed in the Core of each form, and to make the form live accordingly.

It happens sometimes that orbits are narrowed down or even cut in a mundane or Cosmic disaster. Space is full of wreckages which gradually are used as materials for future spirals.

On the human level, the orbits suffer and deteriorate when the Core, in Its ignorance or when forced by outside influences, occupies Itself with hatred, anger, fear, jealousy, revenge, slander, vanity, ego, and separatism.

Such emanations in the orbits disintegrate the electromagnetic field of the spirals.

What will be the correspondences of such pollutants in Cosmic space?

There will be forces, conditions, situations, friction, and attacks in space which will set off a process of disintegration, explosion, or destruction in the spatial bodies. But our astronomers are still unable to discover such parallels between human and universal pollutants.

The pollution in space filters the rays of the Sun. Esoterically, the rays of the Sun stimulate seven centers in our etheric body. If the atmosphere is clean, and the rays reach us through an unobscured space, they nourish equally each center in the head and each center in our higher bodies.

But if space is polluted, the rays cannot reach us in their purity; certain rays cannot reach us at all.

The heartbeat of the Sun sends its rays to our planet. The polluted atmospheric conditions intermittently hinder certain rays from reaching us. Then, when our centers do not receive this nourishment regularly and rhythmically but are fed in an unbalanced way, the chemistry of the rays is not absorbed into our system in its natural purity. Hence, the disturbed state of equilibrium of the mind and health of the entire planet.

For example, we can see this in the idling of our cars. If the gasoline is not properly ignited or if it is polluted, the engine does not do its job because it is fed improperly and with a gasoline that is foreign to the car.

In polluting space, man is on the path of self-destruction. The pollution of space is chemical and psychic.

Psychic pollution is the result of negative emotions, painful and destructive thoughts, crimes and horrors, hatred and malice.

We litter space not only with our poisons and pollutants, but also with our wars, ELF electrical currents, etc. and expect that the currents of light and wisdom, the vitality and beauty coming from the Sun, will reach us.

We are breaking our communication lines with the Life-giver, the Sun. The result will be global disaster if we do not stop polluting space immediately. The accumulated pollution in space will act as conductors or transmitters for certain energies which will have destructive effects on the life-forms.

The spheres around the Earth have specific functions. They balance the intensity of the rays from the Sun, and they either prevent certain currents of energy from reaching Earth or they amplify other currents.

The system of spheres around the Earth is a sensitive organism which acts on behalf of life on Earth. These spheres are like our aura, as they are spheres of energy which either protect the Earth from certain currents or attract certain currents to the Earth. But if the spheres are polluted, the order of nature becomes distorted.

Man has no capacity to prevent the danger of pollution naturally. The increasing pollution has reached such a degree of density that Nature will not be able to recover or regenerate itself.

The rays coming from luminaries are distorted, disturbed, and chemically changed due to accumulated chemicals in the atmosphere.

Thus, the rays or energy currents coming from space will become more dangerous when they mix with massive human hatred, fear, anger, jealousy, and greed. This mixture of the rays and polluted auras of people is responsible for our physical, emotional, and mental illnesses and for the unrest that exists upon the Earth.

Before it is too late, our atmosphere must be cleaned even if it is necessary to work in candlelight or travel on a donkey! To save the life on this planet, no sacrifice is too high.

Toward the year 2000, every human being must pray, think, and work to decrease pollution in any form. It is a known fact that with polluted blood one cannot remain sane, joyful, and healthy.

All our life depends on our *sanity, joy,* and *health.* We cannot afford to destroy the rays of the Sun and change them into rays of death and destruction. We have to leave a beautiful world to our children and to our *children's children.*

How long must humanity wait to hear from scientists that the Universe is a living, conscious Being with a Purpose and a Plan?

How embarrassing it is that some scientists see and analyze the flea on an elephant but are unable to sense and see the elephant itself!

During these few years, great changes and exciting events will take place on many levels or planes simultaneously. Our striving makes us ready to cooperate with the creative power of Nature and enter into the next millennium with victory and glory — and with the realization of One Humanity.

# 8

—•—

# *The Law of Existence*

Killing is always against the Law of Existence. This is a Cosmic Law, and life that comes into existence, especially in human form, must never be destroyed by human hands for any reason. Violation of this Law has been carried out throughout millions of years, creating the most difficult obstacles on the path of human survival. The karma created by killing is so complicated and far reaching that one must do all that is possible not to kill.

Besides the karmic consequences on Earth, there are also complications created in the Subtle World, or the astral world. All horrors of killing, pain and suffering, hatred and revenge are transported there, creating not only an unimaginable terror but also a widespread disturbance and pollution in the Subtle World.

As human astral or emotional disturbances eventually affect the physical body with various diseases, shocks, and attacks, the global astral body will bring a destructive effect on the planetary body in the form of volcanic eruptions, earthquakes, tornadoes, and widespread fires. Still people may think that this is superstition. It is a fact. As the human emotional nature affects his body with various cellular explosions and diseases, so does the global astral nature affect the body of the planet.

Accumulated negative emanations in the sphere of the Earth are responsible for many natural calamities. Such information comes as superstition for the modern man. Very soon, science will prove the relationship existing between holocausts, killings, massive butchering, and natural disasters.

The Ageless Wisdom testifies that every time the Law of Existence is violated by killing, Nature reacts in the form of natural disasters and widespread epidemics.

Those who enter the astral world after their bodies are butchered, mutilated, burned, or evaporated by earthly fires and bombs live in the astral plane like devouring wolves. For a long time they attack human astral bodies, destroying, hurting, or possessing them, to lead them toward insane action, crime, and murder.

These are the "gifts" of war, genocide, and murder which our political or religious leaders offer us age after age, instead of teaching the principles of global cooperation and sharing. After every war, statistics will increasingly show that mental and degenerative diseases spread and flood the population of the Earth.

In the new era, the leaders of nations will act upon the foundation of Brotherhood, sharing, and respecting the Law of Existence. The Law of Existence is the law to exist, the right to exist. And this law will never be violated by any reasoning or any condition.

In the future, the greatest crime will be to try to solve the problems of the world through wars or killing. Instead, people will use their minds, love, and intuition to coexist in freedom, mutual respect, and sharing.

In old cultures, people balanced their behavior by considering the effects of their behavior "above and below," just like today we talk about sickness affecting us psychologically, and thought and emotions affecting us physically.

Every action against the Law of Existence is an action against the Creator, causing delay in His Purpose and Plan as well.

People will argue about how to handle those who murder, kill, destroy, and cause immense suffering to others. The answer is very clear. They must be put in special institutions to be corrected — to be corrected by psychiatric, psychological, philosophical, medical, and religious means. But this action must also be accompanied with an organized effort to prevent the development of the tendency to murder, or the tendency to hurt others for one's own self-interest.

It is not only the murderer who must be corrected but also those who exploit people, manipulate people, or organize legal crimes. Such people often are hidden behind the massive power of money, position, or the military.

Human beings do act against benevolent laws, but the cure is not in killing such people.

If children are educated to be good parents and if parents raise their children in an environment of love, compassion, and consideration for the well-being of others, we will have less and less crime in the world.

Our educational system must be humanized. Great emphasis must be put upon teaching right human relations, goodwill, cooperation, and service.

The economy and the financial condition in the world need fundamental improvement to create an atmosphere of abundance so that people are not tempted to commit crimes.

Literature, movies, and television programs must stop using examples of crime, violence, and destruction. The use of hallucinogenic drugs, marijuana, tobacco, and alcohol must be eradicated and healthy principles must be spread in various ways into every home.

To change the world will take only ten years if all nations cooperate and use their wealth for the rehabilitation of the world, instead of dumping it into the military bucket that has no bottom.

People worry often that unemployment will increase if war machines stop operating. That is the greatest lie ever fabricated. Oceans, mountains, rivers, lakes, deserts, the whole of space are waiting for laborers — if the money for war machines is saved and used to open new, constructive jobs in which the Law of Existence will be strictly observed.

Those who exploit the world will not continue doing so when the fear in their hearts is taken away, and they become convinced that one can be happier in sharing, cooperating, and serving than in exploiting people for various reasons and in various ways.

The New Age or the Golden Age will never come until people learn the sense of right human relationship and resign and renounce old methods of killing and exploiting people for imagined reasons.

# 9

—•—

# *Great Tests*
# *and*
# *Great Opportunities*

Before every New Era, degeneration sets in to such a degree, that it involves physical, emotional, mental, and spiritual realms. As we are approaching the Age of Aquarius, we see widespread degeneration in physical, emotional, mental, and spiritual realms. But this is not all that is happening.

A new generation of thinkers, creative people, and leaders are emerging everywhere in the world. The body of the planet is reacting to the currents of degeneration with currents of fiery spirits who are standing on the creative, constructive, and regenerative path.

Humanity is now like Arjuna[1] between the two armies
— the army that is destroying respect, truth, responsibility,
cooperation, unity, striving, and beauty, and the army that
is standing for the above principles.

In the beginning of every New Era is this natural
phenomenon. The crisis is like a test, like a filter. Those
who cannot pass through it will be thrown out, and those
who pass through it will be facing new, glorious opportunities for development and new achievements.

The crisis now involves every person of every age.
Some people will make it. Some people will be stuck and
degenerate.

The situation being as it is, those who are on the path
of striving will be more alert not to be involved with the
flood of degeneration. They will build their spiritual arks
to protect their spiritual beauty and be the pioneers of the
coming Race. As there are laws by which nations are
controlled and kept in order, so also there are spiritual laws
which, if violated, bring unhappiness and destruction to the
world.

For example, the following are spiritual laws that are
not often discussed in public:

1.  The Law of Beauty

2.  The Law of Harmlessness

3.  The Law of Purity

4.  The Law of Unity

---

1. Warrior depicted in *The Bhagavad Gita*.

5. The Law of Cooperation

6. The Law of Responsibility

7. The Law of Striving Toward Perfection

8. The Law of Love

If these eight laws are violated, the result will be unhappiness, sickness, crime, death, poverty, and misery.

**1. The Law of Beauty.** The ugliness that is going on throughout the world is very powerful. In all fields of human endeavor, you see ugliness facing beauty. Those who are choosing the path of ugliness are violating the path of beauty. Ugliness is expressing itself in the phenomena of crime, violence, murder, unfaithfulness, hatred, exploitation, and in the deformed faces and bodies which are especially shown in movies.

On the other hand, we have in the world masters of beauty who try to reveal our own divinity through their art, painting, music, dance, architecture, and sculpture. They try through their arts to awaken the sense of beauty in people and inspire them to think, feel, and act in the spirit of beauty. They think that beauty not only gives people spiritual satisfaction but also releases the inner potentials of men, organizes their minds, and inspires them to live a life of beauty.

The youth are exposed both to ugliness and beauty. If they choose the path of beauty, if they choose to make their lives beautiful, live in a beautiful environment, try to make the lives of others beautiful, they will be the leaders of the New Age. Otherwise, they will disintegrate and vanish into ugliness.

**2. The Law of Harmlessness**. Harmfulness is everywhere. Children are hurting their parents with their violent nature, uncontrolled behavior, and various involvements. Husbands and wives are hurting each other in many ways and forms every day. Corporations and businesses are hurting people through techniques of manipulation and by various pressures. If one asks who is responsible for the widespread pollution, the poison in Nature, the answer will be: Those who took on the responsibility to take care of people but ignored that responsibility. For example, the states have licensed many activities and businesses that are hazardous for the population.

From childhood, people must learn the Law of Harmlessness, and when they grow, they will exercise the principle of harmlessness in all their decisions and activities. In a sense, the Law of Harmlessness is the Law of Consideration for the welfare of others. Such a law is not discussed properly in kindergartens nor in universities. The violation of such a law will bring disturbances in our families, groups, and nations. It is a great opportunity and a test for all people everywhere to stand for harmlessness and avoid any kind of harmful living. Those who will gradually live a harmless life will in the future shine like bright stars in the life of humanity because they will show humanity the way of beauty, harmlessness, and the economy of energy, time, space, and matter.

Harmful actions, on any level for any purpose, create short-circuits in our system and destroy our happiness in the future. But how can the children of the world develop harmlessness and live a harmless, happy life if every day television, movies, publications, parents, states, and governments are demonstrating the opposite? Only spiritually ready people will be able to resist such a current of crime and try to live a harmless life.

In the past, harmlessness was considered to be the behavior of cowards and of the insane. People will slowly realize that harmlessness is a heroic attitude. Only heroes can be harmless even at the expense of their own lives. Heroism is the synthesis of an expanding consciousness, a sense of direction, responsibility, and of many other virtues. Harmlessness is the crown of the higher level Initiates.

Teaching the Law of Harmlessness to the new generation means to bring a New Age that has a minimum of pain and suffering — an age of happiness, health, success, unity, and joy.

Once a woman told me how cruel her children were, how disrespectful, selfish, and arrogant they were in spite of all her efforts to create a loving heart in them. She concluded, "Whatever good I built in their hearts, the next day it was destroyed by the schools and by television programs and movies, so I gave up." The future of her children was very cloudy, and one could read unhappiness in all their manners.

**3. The Law of Purity** is only partially taught by so-called puritans and fanatics. The purity to which we are referring is the purity of thinking, feeling, and actions.

Pure thinking is a thinking that is not controlled by vanity, egotism, separatism, prejudices, superstitions, or illusions. There is no self-deception in pure thinking.

Pure thinking is not polluted by negative emotions, such as fear, anger, hate, jealousy, revenge, slander, malice, treason, glamors, and so on. Pure thinking is not poisoned by criminal activities such as murder and theft. Pure thinking is charged with feelings of compassion, love, and higher aspiration.

A pure action is not interfered with by posthypnotic suggestions and blind urges and drives. Purity is a state in

which the human soul is in full control of his mechanism
and runs that mechanism in harmony with the Plan and
Purpose of life.

Purity is also related to those actions which are not
involved in crimes of sexual perversion.

**4. The Law of Unity** at present is discussed only by
dreamers or escapists. But this law is one of the basic
foundations upon which all manifestations of life must be
built if people really want to be happy, healthy, prosperous,
and have all the possibilities to conquer and understand the
Universe. Unless there is unity, life will be full of pain and
suffering. Violation of the Law of Unity created all the
suffering and pain that we live in.

This law can be simplified by saying that people must
live a life as if they were one with all life-forms, as if they
were cells in one body, as if all of them had the same urge
to be happy, healthy, prosperous, and enlightened.

Every time we think contrary to the Law of Unity, we
weaken our mental mechanism. Every time we feel separative and selfish, we petrify our heart — that great mechanism of contact with the highest principles of the Universe.
Every time we engage in separative, destructive, and criminal actions, we sow seeds of disease in our body, groups,
and nations because all acts of disunity, momentarily or for
a long time, cut our electrical power from the Cosmic
Source and short-circuit our whole wiring system. Every
time we short-circuit ourselves, we expose ourselves to
viruses, germs, and psychic attacks.

Now the children of the world have a choice to follow
those who daily sow the poisonous seeds of separatism or
to follow those who think, feel, and act in a spirit of unity.
They must remember that unity means order, harmony,

beauty, health, joy, success, and expansion; and disunity means chaos, suffering, and degeneration.

*Isolated Unity* is another concept we must understand.

"Isolated Unity" is a state of consciousness in which you are aware of the One Self in all forms in the whole existence, but you are isolated in space and time due to your individual existence, the limit of your consciousness, and the quantity of your karma. These three elements isolate you naturally from being fused with the whole, but if you are advanced enough in your awareness, you feel one with all that exists.

Isolated unity is a realm in existence, though not many people are aware of it. Such an awareness is a very important achievement as it pressures the person gradually to orchestrate all his thoughts, words, emotions, and actions to be in harmony with the awareness of unity.

If such an awareness is lacking, a person does not have guidance or direction and all his actions are separative and destructive. Such actions conflict with the innate or inherent Law of Unity in Nature and create all those frictions which are the sources of all pain and suffering, as well as personal, social, and planetary upheavals.

The sensed, recognized, inner unity is the guiding star of human life. It is the path which will lead to happiness, health, and prosperity in the world.

Temporary isolation is a way to serve the existing unity. Meditation and retreat are forms of isolation during which you cut all those influences which draw you to the world of differentiations and separatism and focus yourself on a point in your consciousness which is a link between you and the One Self. If your awareness is focused on that unity, then you see a drastic change in your relationships and expressions.

Unity and isolation are the essential phenomena in existence. Unity is a law. Isolation is the manifestation and the multiple creation of that unity into various frequencies and forms. In each form is found the nucleus of unity. Form is a cleavage in homogeneity, but in each form the pilot is the nucleus which eventually takes the existence back to unity through all the thoughts, feelings, words, and actions which are based in unity.

The more we live in an awareness of unity, the closer we go toward the purpose of our life.

The farther we travel from the awareness of unity, the closer we identify ourselves with the process of disintegration, pain, and suffering.

The awareness of unity increases the birth of our consciousness in creativity and success on all planes of existence.

Isolation freezes our consciousness and, as a result, we become involved with various crimes on all planes of our personality existence.

We are told that there will be a great opportunity for us in the year 2000 when the energy of Shamballa will be released once more into the consciousness of humanity, opening further one of the gates of Shamballa, which is symbolically called "The Isolated Unity."[2] This may create an unprecedented cleavage between those who sense that principle of unity and those who stay in the consciousness of isolation or separatism.

One must prepare not only himself but also his group and his nation to be sensitive to that moment of opportunity when a subjective lightning will be released from "the Center where the Will of God is known."

---

2. For further information, please refer to *The Legend of Shamballa*, pp. 59-60.

**5. The Law of Cooperation** is one of the laws that is rarely taught anywhere in the world. Of course, those who stand for the regeneration of the world speak and write about this law everywhere, and those who stand for anarchy and self-interest think and act against the Law of Cooperation by sowing the seeds of selfishness, self-interest, and separatism. This situation is a real test for those who want to survive and live a happy life. Will they be able to propagate the Law of Cooperation and bring integration and synthesis into homes, groups, and nations, or will they let the Law be violated and chaos rule?

Cooperation is one of the basic Cosmic Laws upon which rests all purposeful planetary manifestation. Behind the Law of Cooperation there is Pure Reason, Logic, and Intuitive Perception. Behind the Law of Cooperation there is the vision of global and solar success. Success is a scientific term which means to achieve continuous perfection according to the Purpose planted in each soul.

The success of a programmed disk is to fulfill a job according to its programming. The same is true for each human being. The difference between success and failure is that some of the computer operators are ignorant of how to use the system and the programs, while others know how to use the computers correctly. Cooperation is the ability to know how to use the Supreme Laws of Nature.

At present you see, in films and on television, programs which strongly emphasize ideas against cooperation: between children and parents, between the government and the people, between students and authorities in schools and universities, between the faithful and the church. Such programs teach and propagate how to reject the Law of Cooperation and create chaos among people. The purpose of such activities is to turn people into automatons and take away their right of self-determination. These films and programs urge you to copy their thoughts, their manners, the way they relate to others so that you lose your identity, your reality, and become a tool for the destruction of the Law of Cooperation. In an atmosphere of cooperation, it will be difficult for criminals and opportunists to make their future at the expense of your happiness and health.

**6. The Law of Responsibility** is one of the highest Laws in the Universe. To be responsible means to understand fully that you can make people either happy or miserable by your thoughts, words, and actions. When you have the sense of responsibility, you live in a way that you not only prevent misery for others, but you also increase their joy, happiness, and success and become their protector without violating their freedom.

Parents must teach this law to their children even before they are born. Teachers must always, at every opportunity, teach the Law of Responsibility to their students on all levels.

Friends must remind each other about the Law of Responsibility, and leaders and rulers must understand that they can accomplish their duties only when using the sense of responsibility.

At this time, there are those who stand for the Law of Responsibility. They try not only to live a responsible life but also to inspire responsibility in others. We also have others who try by all means to teach irresponsibility to children and adults, not thinking perhaps that an irresponsible person will be the best customer for prisons, hospitals, and mental institutions. Irresponsibility actually creates income for all sorts of institutions, individuals, and agencies. Many people gain from irresponsibility, a gain that is at the expense of the general good. Why allow irresponsible people to live an irresponsible life at the expense of others?

The fact is that every irresponsible action only shortens your life and makes you live miserably in future incarnations. Every irresponsible act is a hole in your boat and an inflammable material on your long journey.

**7. The Law of Striving Toward Perfection.** There are people all over the world who are against any teaching about striving toward perfection. They teach people just to satisfy their desires, just to satisfy their sexual urges, just to satisfy the urge to use drugs, alcohol, tobacco and so on, and just to be the way they want to be. These are depicted in publications, movies, and television programs which exist everywhere. These people try to tell the youth of the world that they do not need to live a healthy life, they do not need to have a sense of responsibility, they do not need to cultivate virtues and talents, but they need instead to live the way they want.

On the other hand, we have those who try to kindle the flame of striving toward improvement, encouraging us to reach new heights and enter into the path of perfection. Again, the future of humanity is in the hands of those who choose discipline — the path of striving toward improvement and perfection.

It is very simple to understand that it is the accumulation of energy and the proper use of time and space that bring the greatest success and the greatest results in our life. A machine that is leaking energy, a wire that has a short-circuit, a bucket that is cracked, a tube that is burned out can accomplish very little in life. But there are people who, in an organized way, discourage every kind of discipline and planned striving for improvement. It is a challenge, for those who are smart enough, to turn their backs on such degenerative activities and collect all their time, energy, and resources to forge ahead toward the betterment of their lives.

When a vision is not given to the youth, the youth cannot strive, and wherever there is no striving, there will be decay.

**8. The Law of Love** is one of the most important laws in the Universe and that is why there are organized activities to make people misunderstand and misuse that law.

For a great number of people, to love means to have sex without commitment and responsibility. To those ends, all pornographic literature and movies are organized to catch people in such a degree that they could not see any other meaning in love.

Children are exposed to every kind of love in movies and television programs. Prematurely, their sex centers are over-stimulated to such an extent that they will sacrifice their parents and other values and even their futures to have sex. Premature sex leaves them unsatisfied, depressed, pregnant, with sexually transmitted diseases, in crises, and in hatred. Most of them lose their self-respect and are involved in unending problems which they cannot possibly solve.

On the other hand, there are people who teach the true meaning of love — in sex, in marriage, in family or cooperative labor, in heroic acts, and even in aspiration, devotion, and dedication to higher visions. They say to us that love is not only the satisfaction of sexual needs but also the understanding of responsibility. Love even acts as sacrifice, as firm friendship. There are people who demonstrate their love in helping you reach your vision, in protecting you from dangers, in helping you build a successful future, in cooperating with you in your plans. These people bring discoveries and ideas by which all of humanity will step into the age of true Brotherhood.

Again, the world presents to us two paths — a path that eventually will lead humanity to degeneration and disease, and a path that will lead humanity to ever glorious summits of love.

Love is the revealer of divinity, glory, and vision. Why not teach our children how to love, instead of how to waste their energies prematurely and end up in hospitals and asylums! The responsibility is ours. The choice is theirs.

Many children will burn their chakras due to misuse, and for many lives they will damage their health and risk their happiness. Many children will burn their wings by entering the sphere of a Teaching which is far too advanced for them.

Only a minority of children will be able to escape the traps on their path set by movies, television, publications, and by the negative examples of their parents and teachers. Only these shielded ones will be able to enter into the Path of striving toward perfection. These are the children who will be the leaders in the coming Race.

These children, though few in number in comparison to the multitudes, will demonstrate leadership abilities in politics, education, the science of communication, the arts, in pure science, religion, and economy and will bring in changes to prepare these seven fields of human endeavor to be the foundation for the coming Race.

These children will have a tough life, a difficult and dangerous life, but because of their physical, emotional, and mental purity and their spiritual striving, they will be able to change all adverse conditions in their lives into assets and resources of wisdom.

All difficulties in their lives will multiply their efforts to conquer their limitations and strengthen their will to achieve. But, of course, the majority of the children of the world will perish in sexually transmitted diseases, drugs, alcohol, smoking, hate, anger, jealousy, malice, and revenge.

Those who are ready to help the children of the world will be divided into the following three sections:

1. Those who will guide the gifted children who have a vision into those efforts which will economize their energy, time, and body and keep their vision burning brightly.

2. Those who will make every kind of effort to liberate the children who are mixed with darkness and light, with aspiration and depression. Even though they may be caught in various traps, they will appreciate any help that will release them from such traps. The helpers of these children will have a difficult time but, in the meantime, will learn great lessons.

3. Those who will follow the steps of the lost and wounded sheep and will study the reasons why they were lost, what can be done to help them, and how to put into their hearts the sparks of hope. Such efforts will not be lost, and thousands of years later the planted fiery seed will cause miracles in these children's lives.

Leaders in the educational field will prepare their workers to be volunteers in such a Herculean labor. The currents of darkness and destruction and the currents of light and regeneration are in a fierce fight. It is imperative that all enlightened people offer their energy to light, to make the darkness retreat.

It is noticed that those children who are in the second and third categories display intelligence, cunning, and logic and talk about freedom and independence in order to fool those who try to help them. If you observe them closely, you will see that their intelligence is serving their desires and vices. Their logic is a device of deception, and freedom for them means license. They hate discipline, service, respect, and gratitude. They are always ready to receive money and various kinds of help, but they themselves do not like to put their lives in order, nor do they like to serve others, helping them to a happier life. The third category, especially, hates authorities, parents, teachers, and advisors and rushes down the path of self-destruction.

Educators often plan various methods to help children when they are already in trouble. The best time to help children is when they are in the womb of their mother.

Educators must prepare special courses for pregnant mothers and encourage them to attend these courses. Then they should prepare a course which will be given to the children from birth to five years old. Such a curriculum will be the best way to save the future children and bring them into the sphere of light, happiness, health, success, and prosperity of the New Age.[3]

In all these courses, the eight laws must be taught in a gradient degree. Those who will go through such courses will be the engineers of the new life on the planet.

These eight laws are laws of survival and laws of success, health, and happiness. Eventually great thinkers will come and put all these eight laws into music, into dance, into paintings, and into science to make humanity live

---

3. For further information, please refer to *Woman, Torch of the Future* and *Sex, Family, and the Woman in Society*.

according to these laws. It is at that time that the real New Age will open its gates of glory for the future of humanity.

All men everywhere must transform this planet, must make efforts to change the thinking of the people, must make efforts to change the way we relate to each other. Let us greet the sun of the first day of the year 2000 with a deep realization of the Brotherhood of Humanity.

# 10

———•———

## *Expectation*

What can we expect if, toward the year 2000, humanity makes itself ready to respond to the energy of the Tower, to the energy of the Father's Home?

First, let us discuss *readiness*.

In this case, the readiness of humanity will appear first as a global feeling that all humanity has the right to live in a safe world, in happiness, and in prosperity.

The second phase of readiness will appear as a global understanding that territorial disputes and territorial borders are insignificant if people live together, if everyone respects the rights of other people to live and to be prosperous, safe, and happy.

The third phase of readiness will appear as a global understanding that unless we appreciate each other's existence and differences, we cannot reach a synthesis.

These three phases of readiness are the three steps to enter into the gate of the year 2000.

What can we expect if humanity is ready to respond to the incoming energy of Life, the energy of the more abundant Life?

The first expectation is that the population of the world, charged with that energy, will declare that the leaders of humanity will do the following:

1. Live for the people of the Earth, for all life-forms existing on Earth.

2. Live for the integration and synthesis of humanity on this globe.

3. Transform all weapons into usable devices to further the happiness and health of humanity.

4. Be those who will have direct contact with the guiding purpose of human life on this planet and be able to orchestrate the life on this Earth accordingly.

5. Eliminate the fear of punishment in any form and create safety by eliminating all causes leading to destructive action.

Second, the educators of the world will create methods to call into action all latent virtues and potentials in man and orient him into creative actions.

Education has been an effort to increase intelligence, knowledge, and technology in all fields. The education of the future will work with the will aspect of man, with his beingness, rather than make him accumulate knowledge and create methods of destruction.

Education will prove how beingness is superior to knowledge and possessions.

Third, those who are engaged in the labor of communication will create colleges and universities in which people will cultivate spiritual telepathy, which in two-hundred years may replace television, telephones, and radios — thus saving the world from various pollutants.

Fourth, the artists of the world will engage themselves in creating beauty and evoking the beauty in each man through all kinds of art forms. Art will turn into a means of communication with the unseen world.

Fifth, the scientists of the world will discover the secrets of perpetual motion, the laws that will free people from the central gravity and give them power to travel without mechanical means. In three to four hundred years, all our transportation machines will rest in museums as a witness to our past ignorance and greed.

Scientists will discover the existence of the human soul, and people will live as streams of light, love, and beauty.

The Twenty-First Century will be called the "Century of the Sun," as the sun will replace all electrical industry and mechanical industry. We do not need to harness the energy of the atom. The greatest reactor and atomic plant in the Solar System is the sun. We need only to use its energy. What has been done thus far to use solar energy is a very small percentage compared to what can be done in the future.

The sun energy will not only be used for lighting, heating, cooling, and operating small machinery, but it will also be used in agriculture, in massive constructions, communication, healing, increasing our intelligence, and expanding our consciousness.

The sun energy will be used for food in concentrated forms, like pills or capsules. Man will eat sun-energy. This

energy contains seventy-seven original colors which will be
used to create corresponding sound waves.

Science will be occupied for a long time with the
cleaning of forms from distortion, disturbances, and poisons. The planet will be made ready for a divine marriage.

Sixth, religion will change a great deal. Man will
worship man in order to worship the Creator. Religion will
be a way of direct communication with Those Forces and
Lives in the Universe Who supervise the manifestation
according to the Supreme Will.

Seventh, the economists of the world will teach us about
the abundance we have within us and show us how to use
that abundance to bring happiness and joy.

Poverty, disease, greed, hatred, punishment, and imposition will no longer exist. People will be cured by the
rays of the Luminaries and by the medicine found in Space.

People will live as long as they want, maybe two to
three hundred years. But as their contact with the Higher
Worlds increases, they will discard their physical bodies
and vest themselves with planetary, solar, and galactic
bodies.

The year 2000 is the dawn of the future. Those who
live for the future are invincible, and they will be the ones
who will have the permission to share the glory of existence.

Thus suppression, exploitation, and manipulation will
fade away, along with all methods of taxation.

Everything will be so abundant that people will not
think about how to exploit people. Increasingly, abundance
will annihilate the importance of money and, with it, the
power of greed.

Every action of the leaders who work against the
Common Good will meet with the irresistible resistance of
the people.

The power will be in the hands of people, and the energy of the Tower will not allow any division in people.

Great heroes in the past had great dreams for their personal life, for their group and nation. The true heroes in the future will be those who will dream for the future of humanity, and they will be ready to burn their lives on the flames of those dreams.

The door of initiation to the new life will have two diamond pillars upon which the ark of the New Era will rest: **Future** and **Beauty**.

No one will pass through these two pillars without transforming his nature through *Future* and *Beauty*.

It is not a secret that close to the year 2000 or 2050 major geographical changes will occur in Africa, Europe, and America. Those changes will occur because of the karma of our past. But human calamities can be minimized if all the people in the world create the Brotherhood of Humanity, decide to walk the path of righteousness, and respond to the energy to be released in the year 2000 at the Wesak Full Moon. These geographical changes will wipe out millions of lives and bring a new civilization into being.

Imagine what will happen if one-third of the continents submerge into the ocean. It is said that national catastrophes are the result of distorted human thinking, greed, hatred, and destructive action.

Still we have time to stop the global madness and enter into the rhythm of Nature.[1]

A human being has a great power over Nature — whether he is conscious of it or not. Being an active mechanism in the energy currents of the Universe, he can

---

1. For further explanation, please refer to *Cosmic Shocks*.

cause various changes in these currents, changes which may result in destruction or rejuvenation.

There are great powers in man which act as keys to manipulate these energy currents. An electrical switch is a small mechanism, but it can put into action the machine of a great factory or stop it.

The human being is a switch, controlled by his thoughts, visualizations, imaginations, words, and actions.

Earthquakes are controlled by energy currents. Disturbances in these currents may have drastic effects on the continents.

Even an evil man can switch on and off the currents on which the whole world exists.

It is time to direct human thought to the five pointed star — Beauty, Goodness, Righteousness, Joy, and Freedom — to save the world from future catastrophes.

The year 2000 is a door of superior opportunity. Future historians will remember the date — *the year 2000, the Wesak Full Moon* — as the originator of all rhythms which will lead to a Super Era, if humanity responds to the call of global Brotherhood.

# 11

—•—

## *Regeneration*

Regeneration starts after a good rest during which the seed, the person, or the group accumulates and concentrates its energies to start once more its creative cycles on an even higher spiral.

We see how Nature does the same. After a good winter rest, spring comes with new flowers, leaves, waterfalls, and with songs of birds and beauty.

This is true on every level — for our body, heart, and soul; for our relationships, creativity, and service. Regeneration must be very inclusive. Nature in all its forms exhausts its energies, then rests and regenerates itself.

During the period of rest, all fall into their right places. The mechanism is repaired, and the spirit is charged with new challenges for new days.

In every regenerative effort, we feel as if someone is waiting for us. It can be someone; it can be an ideal, a dream, a vision, or the future. The seed sleeping within us, in "winter," dreams about the flower it is going to be.

During every regenerative effort, we have a similar dream that inspires us to make every effort to achieve it.

Regeneration is a process of resurrection. This process demands labor, effort, and striving. Regeneration is also the process by which you destroy your limitations.

You see how a nutshell is destroyed before a new plant comes out of the earth. In each effort of regeneration, some limitations must be destroyed. Most of these limitations are psychological and mental crystallizations which, curiously enough, contain all the potential seeds of regeneration.

Regeneration must be experienced in your entire nature, and you will have that experience only through actualizing your regeneration through all your relationships. Regeneration must bring its fruits if it is real, if it is factual.

Often you must ask yourself, "What effort am I making to surpass myself? What effort am I making to expand my consciousness? What am I doing to be more soul, less personality in my relationships? Do I have contacts with Higher Worlds? What is the proof? Am I satisfied with knowledge, with objects, rather than with the process of actualization?"

You may ask such questions of yourself and seek answers.

The Chalice, which is the Treasury of our life, can cause regeneration in our physical, emotional, and mental bodies if it is filled with the spirit of our sincerity, effort, labor, and striving.

Regeneration manifests through the fruits of our labor and the fruits in our daily relationships — fruits of nobility, gracefulness, tenderness, orderliness, sincerity, simplicity, peace, creativity, patience, endurance, success, and achievements. Without fruits, how can we be sure that we are involved in the process of regeneration?

Regeneration means, also, continuously to destroy our old images and build new ones which are more adaptable for higher contacts, communication, and creativity.

When you are crystallized in your former image, you cannot regenerate yourself. Each crystallized image has its own limitation. For example, one such limitation is, "I can't be successful."

Another is, "I can't have a nice husband, wife, or children. That is my destiny."

Others are

— "I can't learn."

— "I can't talk."

— "I can't improve."

— "All that I am, I am satisfied with."

— "I am always sick, defeated, and failing."

— "People don't like me."

— "I am ugly and unattractive."

Such images are cemented in our mind, and they prevent us from regenerating ourselves. One of the important steps in regeneration is to destroy our old self-image. We can destroy our old image by first knowing it as it is through observation, and then aspiring and striving for a new image.

Most of our self-images are like a coffin which entombs our dead spirit. This spirit must be resurrected. Our self-image controls the quality of our thoughts, our emotional expressions, our health, and our physical activities. By

changing our self-image, we change all that we are doing
or not doing on all levels of our personality.

Once we build a self-image that is not progressive,
increasingly searching and inclusive, we crystallize
ourselves.

Once my father said to a person, "Unless your inner
sun melts away the ice of your self-image, there will be no
regeneration for you." Regeneration needs the awakening
of the *seed*.

The spirit that is within us and in Nature always
regenerates itself. Pain and suffering occur when we create
hindrances for its regeneration; joy and happiness emerge
when we allow the spirit to expand and regenerate itself.

All ideological, religious, and scientific fanaticism
leads us to crystallization, and when the spirit starts to
regenerate itself, pain and suffering result because of our
crystallization.

In the Teaching we read about living corpses which
cannot regenerate themselves and stay for a long time as
they are. Such corpses are more dangerous because not only
do they pollute space physically, but they also pollute the
environment with their emotions and thoughts and prevent
people from making new breakthroughs in their life.

One of the obstacles to regeneration is the accumulation
of your harmful actions, feelings, words, and thoughts.
Whoever is harmful has a very slight chance to regenerate
himself. Harmfulness destroys the seed that was intended
to sprout. Harmfulness increases your karma, and it is such
karma that prevents you from regenerating yourself. If your
life is full of harmful actions, you will have enormous
difficulties in regenerating yourself.

Spiritual regeneration can also be possible if you know
how to *rest*. Esoterically, rest means to withdraw yourself
within the sphere of light, love, and power of your Soul; to

withdraw yourself into your vision, ideas and future and spread your roots into such spheres so that when the time of labor comes, you start flourishing with creativity and glory. Regeneration is not possible unless your roots penetrate into higher spheres of Beauty, Goodness, Righteousness, Joy, and Freedom.

Rest is a withdrawal, a retreat into your True Self — as far as it is possible for you to do that.

It is possible that you can even "rest" while you are occupied with your daily activities and draw regenerative energies from your Inner Self.

Other obstacles to our regeneration are

— Glamors

— Attachments

— Identifications

Glamors are all our condensed desire forms surrounding our emotional body.

Attachments are on all levels, and that to which we are attached makes us the victim of that object. That object sucks all our energy, or a major part of it.

Identification is a bigger obstacle because, with whatever we identify ourselves, we *lose* ourselves in that object and become that object itself.

If you observe yourself, you may see that every time you are caught in your glamors, attachments, and identifications, you feel depressed to a large or small degree. A depressed person hardly has a chance to regenerate himself. Lord Buddha strongly emphasizes the need for *detachment* because detachment allows you to regenerate yourself, and there is no spiritual life without constant regeneration.

Nature sometimes imposes detachment to bring in a new regeneration. In the forms of natural cataclysms, earthquakes, devastating fires, tornadoes, floods, etc., it takes away from people all to which they were attached. Usually after every disaster you see a new process of regeneration. All leaves must go so that the tree ornaments itself with new leaves and new branches, and with new aspirations.

Let us discuss some practical steps for regeneration:

1. Every day try to jump rope, jump on a trampoline, or do some other good physical activity.

2. Be joyful and humorous without being hilarious. Try to laugh, tell jokes, humorous stories or anecdotes. Joyfulness has a great regenerative effect on your whole system. Not only can you regenerate yourself with humor and joy, but humor and joy are also the best means to regenerate others.

You can humorously show people how they act or behave under depression, and they will immediately feel relief. Laughter regenerates you and others. Laughter is sometimes like the lightning which disperses darkness. Laughter pulls in energy from your Solar Angel. Actually, the Solar Angel could not stay with us if It could not laugh about the many stupid things we do.

3. The next step is to have a daily contact with your vision. Your vision is that which you aspire to be. Make your vision high, inclusive, harmless, beautiful, but not impossible. Impossible dreams can depress you if you feel that they are out of your reach.

Every true vision is a part of your true archetype. To have a vision means to be in contact with your regenerative source — the archetype. No matter where your vision is on the scale of life, it imparts to you regenerative energy. The difference between people is the difference in how close they are to their vision. Even if you have a little vision but are close to it, you are more advanced than another person whose vision is in the sky and he does not try to actualize it.

4. The next step is to have rhythm. To have rhythm means subjectively to feel and follow the rhythms of the Core of Nature. Synchronization with Nature can have a tremendous regenerative effect on your system.

The rhythm of the sun and stars, the rhythms of the regenerative energies of Nature, the beauty, joy and freedom, all these can regenerate your system if you tune into them.

Rhythm is a measured step of expansion and contraction, inhalation and exhalation, rest and expression. Regeneration is possible when the rhythm of your body, emotions, and thoughts harmonizes itself with the rhythm of your Soul.

5. The next step is increasing your joy. Joy has a great effect in the regenerative process. It is observed that joyfully conceived and raised children have an immense capability for regeneration on all levels.

Joy increases when you share it or give it to others. The joy that you give to others comes back to you with the highest interest. Actually, there is no true joy other than the joy you plant in others. Limiting joy to one's self even leads you to crimes. Plant seeds of joy in others and your harvest of joy will be overwhelming. Beauty, freedom, and enlightenment are sources of joy. Rhythmic actions, rhythmic meditations, and rhythmic speech bring joy.

6. Service creates regenerative energy in your system. If you want to regenerate yourself, try to serve others without expectation and slowly expand the field of your service. Thus the energy created can be used for regeneration.

7. Sincerity and simplicity bring in regenerative energy. The more simple and sincere you are, the more energy you have.

Insincerity blocks the currents of regenerative energy and creates conflicting forces within you.

Simplicity protects you from artificiality which can create great obstacles on the path of your regeneration.

8. Regeneration can also be possible when you make real efforts to make contact with your psychic energy, with your Soul, with your Teacher, or study his works of Wisdom. It is a great privilege to have a Teacher and be inspired by him. It makes a great difference in your life.

There are higher sources of inspiration for which not all of us are ready. For example, the Hierarchy is a great source of inspiration. Shamballa is a greater source for regenerative energies. Eventually we can contact these sources if we keep the process of our regeneration active.

9. Regeneration is also caused by the achievement of other people. Anyone who achieves spiritually releases and channels a tremendous amount of energy which kindles our centers and stimulates our soul to change things in our life.

"I call you from refreshment to labor," a Master once said. Refreshment is reading, writing, learning. Labor is the process of using all that you have accumulated in practical work and service.

# $Q_{\&}A$

**Question:** _How can we exercise daring and use it to regenerate ourselves?_

**Answer:**

— By learning that spiritual values are more important than physical values

— By learning to sacrifice our money, body, ego, and vanity to preserve spiritual values

— By developing fearlessness, detachment, concentration, and dedication to spiritual principles

— By developing contact with our Solar Angel

— Through meditation, because continuous meditation makes us realize that all forms, including our bodies and possessions, are not real and that we can sacrifice them to reach our destination in daring

— By coming in contact with our Master

— By having a powerful love for the principles for which we dare

The difference between courage and daring is that in courage you do not risk but in daring you risk. Courage is the power of the soul to make you perform important deeds. Daring makes you a hero. A hero risks all that he has and is. He becomes a hero only through sacrifice.

Spiritual means ever-progressing, advancing, expanding onward movement.

Daring means to do things risking your

1. Body

2. Position

3. Possessions

4. Comfort

to move your beingness forward on the path of your regeneration.

**Question:** *How do I handle people who slander me when I try to serve them?*

**Answer:** Well, the first thing to know is that slandering is the method of hiding oneself from open and secret crimes. Those who slander want to cover all that they did to harm others. They are full of poison, and they want to get rid of it. Hence, they slander others.

The second thing is to try to live a better life so as not to give a chance to the slanderer.

Third, never react to them because the Law of Karma will handle them at the proper time. In my entire life, I have never seen a person happy who is occupied with gossip and slander. Their life is always miserable.

**Question:** *How do we really harm people?*

**Answer:** There are two ways that we harm people:

1. Not letting them improve, develop, and unfold

2. Letting them unfold and be enlightened

The first one is selfish and based on various interests. The second one is sacrificial, risky, but pleasant to God.

**Question:** *Does Nature cause regeneration within our nature?*

**Answer:** Yes. Cyclically, Nature releases regenerative forces, but these forces do not regenerate us unless we cooperate with them. Regeneration is based on our responses to these forces and our own efforts, aspirations, and striving.

# 12

———•———

## What is Success?

The meaning of success changes as your consciousness expands and your beingness travels toward perfection.

Success is related to your free will. Whenever you control something or conquer something, you translate that as a success. You can control and conquer yourself physically, emotionally, and mentally and call yourself a successful man. Also you can control and conquer others physically, emotionally, and mentally and think you are a successful man.

Success is also related to the accumulation of many objects. The more you accumulate, the more you think you are successful. Havingness is the result of competition.

Unfortunately, most of our successes are based on the failure of others. After such success, people still feel that they are missing something very essential. They feel their success has left them empty and unsatisfied.

Sometimes this emptiness and dissatisfaction lead them to take extreme measures by taking revenge on themselves in the form of suicide or in the form of various actions which result in a miserable physical, emotional, and mental condition.

When success is translated as victory over others, a person does almost anything to gain superiority in order to perpetuate his victory. But again, the void in him expands with each step of such a victory.

What is this vacuum that can never be filled with any kind of success or any kind of victory? In the future, the words "success" and "victory" will be considered crimes — because success and victory have been related to the defeat and failure of others.

The human essence cannot tolerate a success achieved at the expense of others, or a victory achieved by the defeat of others. As long as the "others" are not equally successful or victorious — the vacuum deepens in the heart of those who think about themselves as victorious and successful people.

The passing of years, the accumulation of degrees and positions of power cannot make a person understand such a subtle concept. A person must make a breakthrough into higher realms of the Cosmic Mind to understand this concept and to discover the medicine with which to heal his vacuum.

Success and victory are based on ego, vanity, self-interest, and separatism as long as success and victory belong to a particular person, group, or nation. Any success that does not help others to be successful, any victory that does not make others victorious is a failure and a defeat in the long run.

Real success is the success of global humanity. Any true victory is the victory of humanity. Any success achieved by the defeat of others is in itself a failure. Maybe it is a failure of intelligence, maybe a failure of heart, maybe a failure in compassion, or a failure in communication. Our present civilization is heading toward destruction in urging people to be successful and victorious at the expense of others. Every such success is the beginning of a failure. Every such victory is the beginning of a defeat.

Instead of urging people to gain success for their own use, we can teach them how to be really successful by trying to help others be successful. Instead of boasting about their victory, we can make people victorious over the limitations that they have, over the separatisms which they cherish, over the ignorance in which they are lost, over the diseases which they spread.

Every spiritually advanced person must live for all humanity and develop his potentials just to help humanity. This will be a true success if achieved. We destroy the future of groups and nations when we teach them to orchestrate their lives in separative pursuits — encouraging them to manipulate and exploit others for their own advantage.

Then the great question comes: how to deal with those who really want to destroy us?

Wars never resolve animosities. Instead, there are several steps we can take:

1. Know that they are "us," and these are past accounts between "us."

2. Open a dialogue, and in all sincerity protect the rights of others and make them see your own rights.

3. Teach the idea that the world belongs to all of us, and we must benefit from the world as one humanity.

4. Eradicate the borders of all nations.

5. Teach that true religion is right human relationship, goodwill, true love, and sacrificial service.

6. Show how the money wasted in wars can be used to educate people in the vision of an advancing humanity.

7. Increase the numbers of advanced psychologists, and make people pass through tests to serve in higher positions. The tests are proficiency in and the manifestation in daily life of

  — The Law of Unity

  — Sacrificial Service

  — Solemnity

  — Harmlessness

8. Do not contaminate the people of other nations with a future vision of military victory. Such nations arm themselves to take revenge on you, or take revenge on other nations.

Every kind of war, even ones fought to "solve" problems, is an attack on the welfare of humanity as a whole.

There are no holy wars or just wars. War is the result of insanity and the weakness of diplomacy.

The world never advanced on the path of love, understanding, health, happiness, and beauty through wars.

Those whom you killed will kill you in the future.

If wars are continued, it will result in wiping humanity totally from this planet.[1]

Rearmament is the curse of victory, and rearmament is the cause of the next war. Intelligent people will not tolerate such an insanity.

No success, no victory is valid unless it is a success or victory for all humanity on this globe.

---

1. For information on the effect of wars in the Higher Worlds, please refer to *Other Worlds*; check index under War, Battle.

# 13

———•———

# *New Diplomacy*

Diplomacy is the science of negotiation used to eradicate the ill will among nations and establish right relations among them.

People cannot learn to be real diplomats unless they have inclusiveness, compassion, and a deep understanding of human nature.

Diplomacy is a science. True diplomatic activities should be based on the criteria of

1. Understanding people

2. Cooperating with people's higher goals

3. Enabling people to see our own real motives and goals

4. Helping to create in others ever-expanding viewpoints

5. Securing the existence and freedom of others and providing the ways and means for their physical and emotional well-being

6. Providing the greatest possible education so that everyone is able to understand cooperation, responsibility, and an ever-inclusive world order

7. Evoking a sense of beauty in others

Diplomacy has not followed these criteria. Rather, it has been based on

— Exploitation

— Manipulation

— Suppression

— Threat

— Force

Such a diplomacy has been used for thousands of years, causing never ending pain, suffering, destruction, and animosity. It is known that pain, suffering, destruction, and animosity are currents of forces which will meet those who caused them in the next cycle. However, after many generations these currents can exhaust themselves if new fuel is not added to them.

We must create schools of diplomacy which will teach the science of real diplomacy. This science can be taught only by those who have understanding and experience regarding three important subjects:

1. Destiny and the vision of life

2. The paradigm formed by such a vision

3. The world of thoughts, ideas, and intentions

Without being trained in these three subjects, a man cannot be a true diplomat, and his activities, instead of creating harmony and cooperation, create animosity and antagonism; instead of creating the common good, create self-interest and exploitation; instead of creating under-standing and right human relations, create confusion and wars.

Diplomacy cannot create a lasting peace, prosperity, and happiness if, behind the diplomacy, there exist separa-tive interests, motives of exploitation, and the desire to control. In diplomacy, the interests of all parties and their rights must be considered and must form the basic platform for discussion.

Diplomacy with enemies must be carried out on the platform of true respect.

A true diplomat, before reacting against the enemy, tries to enter into the enemy's shoes and understand as clearly as possible the reasons for the enemy's actions.

Understanding comes first. The influence of the enemy's actions upon humanity, nations, and the future should be considered next. Understanding of these factors will help diplomats to clarify the issues with so-called enemies.

Enemies often act, as we do, like single human beings who are under the control of their blind urges and drives,

post-hypnotic suggestions, and dark forces. They need
psychological or psychiatric help, devoid of exploitative or
manipulative motives.

It is easy to confront an enemy with weapons and arms,
but it is more beneficial to cure the enemy. Often we cannot
cure an enemy because we are our own enemies, hiding our
motives and intentions, or demonstrating our will to destroy
these so-called enemies.

True diplomacy is impersonal. That is what is lacking
in modern diplomacy.

Everyone's diplomacy is based on his self-interest.
There is no true diplomacy in self-interest. This means,
then, that all the diplomacy carried out upon the stage of
politics is a comedy and a tragedy.

The purpose of diplomacy is to cure cleavages and
establish right human relations, no matter what the costs are
for the interested parties. Seen objectively, this cost will be
insignificant in comparison to the cost that animosity can
create.

Diplomacy also has to follow the Law of Economy,
creating a system of economy which is acceptable to all
people, not only governments, because certain governments
are the enemies of their people and they do not really
represent the people in their diplomacy.

The existence of cleavages among the nations proves
the bankruptcy of diplomacy in the world.

The economic situation in the world is another proof
that diplomacy as a whole has been a form of greed and
exploitation, instead of a course of wise action taken for the
benefit of all.

Diplomats very often are the puppets of governments.
No puppet can do a creative job.

Diplomatic actions have also been based on the reports
of spies. Spying is a tolerated activity in our diplomacy.

Instead of sincerity and openness, nations spy and steal from each other. It is also deplorable that diplomats encourage such activities. They cheat each other and keep their relations with each other in order to continue and further their cheating.

Such immoral actions, demonstrated on the stage of the world, are bad examples for all peoples of the world.

Diplomacy is the science of relationship. When governments demonstrate double-faced diplomacy based on dishonesty, they cause degeneration in the morals of nations. Once the morals of nations degenerate, governments use force to bring people "into order." It is known that the use of force is the final sign of the bankruptcy of a government's diplomacy.

If a thorough research is done on a world-wide scale, proof will be found to show that a nation's morality degenerates due to a dishonest, wasteful, bureaucratic, and totalitarian government.

It is known that the diplomacy of rulers does not degenerate if their morality is of the highest caliber. Social injustice is a great sign that shows the bankrupt morality of the government.

Diplomacy until now — and who knows how long it will last — has been based on separative interests. This is the first point that must be recognized. Future diplomacy must be based not only on the mutual rights of interested parties but also on the rights of all people everywhere. Imposition of diplomacy through many forms of suppression is a game that will bring pain and sorrow.

The new diplomacy will never act through fear, threat, and suppression, but it will even try to eliminate all traces of fear, threat, and suppression. As long as fear, threat, and suppression exist, there will be no lasting cooperation, harmony, understanding, and peace.

Actually, the existence of armies is proof that the leaders of humanity have not been able to use their brains but are instead victims of their vanity, ego, self-interest, and separatism. Most of these leaders have been obsessed by fear, anger, jealousy, and revenge and have been acting under the dominance of such vices. But, alas, people regard them as national heroes.

The most horrible thing is that successive leaders have continued to follow the policies of their predecessors. Seldom does a government come into existence that corrects the mistakes committed by the former government. Instead, the new government often justifies the crimes of the former, thus perpetuating the effects of past misdeeds. Often leaders may even attack certain past policies just to continue them behind the scenes.

Humanity is now anxious to see its leaders create a world that is safe, a world that is organized in such a way that there is universal understanding and harmony, a world in which there are no homeless and hungry people, a world that is enlightened by the beauty of real education.

Of course, such a world will still have problems and difficulties due to past actions, but the real diplomats will be able to solve these problems for the good of all.

It is the hope of humanity that the ideal diplomats will appear after the year 2000, cause real transformation in the relationships of people, and change the ways of diplomatic relations — after repeating each other's mistakes for such a long time.

# 14

—•—

## *Ages*

Historians have divided the planetary periods into various "ages," such as the Stone Age, Iron Age, Brass Age, etc. However, these names do not give the true character of these ages.

Real ages are states of consciousness, not states of phenomena. We can therefore give the following names to various planetary periods, according to the development of consciousness:

1. The animal age, or animal age consciousness

2. The age of human mass mentality, herd consciousness, or crowd and homogeneous consciousness

3. The age of individuality

4. The age of groupings

5.  The age of nations

6.  The age of humanity

7.  The age of planetary consciousness

These ages never end. Like wheels within each other, they turn with bright colors or become faint, thus affecting each other continuously and producing the life on the planet which we call history.

The *first stage* is the consciousness of animal man, standing confused in his own existence. He hardly separates himself from the phenomena of Nature and lives as a wave in the currents of the forces of Nature.

The *second stage* is the human mass age in which man knows that there is a difference between himself and Nature, but still he is involved in mass consciousness and lives as a wave in the ocean of the mass.

The *third stage* starts when man kindles his mental fire, begins to separate himself from the masses, and lives as an individual. He is selfish; he tries to survive at the expense of others. He lives for himself.

In the *fourth stage* of consciousness, man begins to form his group: a family group and children, a group which he owns. He forms his group of people to secure his existence and to fight against other groups to perpetuate his dominance over others.

The *fifth stage* of consciousness begins when human beings outgrow the grouping consciousness and expand it into a national consciousness in which the idea of a nation and race play the prominent role. A nation is the higher correspondence of the stage in which the individual worships himself and lives for himself at the expense of others.

In the *sixth stage* of consciousness, the nations slowly melt away and form united kingdoms or united states and, instead of nations, humanity begins to act as one humanity.

In the *seventh stage* of consciousness, humanity strongly fuses with the consciousness of the planet, and a planetary consciousness emerges in which humanity feels one with the life of the planet. This is the correspondence of the first age on a higher spiral.

Every progress toward a higher state of consciousness may need millions of years of crises, problems, destructions, and family emancipations. World history is the faintest recordings of such crises and achievements.

Each higher state of consciousness can be achieved by the destruction of the limitations of the former state of consciousness.

But we must be aware that all these stages of consciousness, on all levels, exist continuously in different magnitudes. The whole movement toward a global consciousness is so powerful that the ages function as parts of one mechanism playing different roles.

It is known that many destructive wars and cataclysms occurred on this earth whenever people could not destroy their prisons and step forward to the next stage of consciousness. Nature uses cataclysms in many forms to assist humanity to expand its consciousness into new dimensions. Of course, between the cataclysm and the point of equilibrium of consciousness on a new dimension, thousands of ages pass until the new level becomes a natural level of consciousness.

We are living now in the age of nations. This will last many decades until we realize that we are not separate nations but one humanity. This is when the new and supreme age will dawn within our consciousness.

People think that it is a specific point in time that makes an age. But in reality, it is the consciousness that makes an age.

The ever-changing configurations of stars are the source of ages. But an age does not come about until the majority of human beings at that time respond to such changes, and respond to the different chemistry in Space through their consciousness.

Configurations of stars can do very little positive change unless human consciousness responds to such configurations. But changing configurations can cause cataclysms in various forms when human consciousness reacts or does not respond to such configurations.[1]

Real cycles, or ages, are produced and affirmed by human consciousness, and each age is an age of consciousness.

Changes that are forced on human beings do not bring new ages. But changes brought on by human consciousness can create new and refined forms. A higher age is the result of the cooperation of human consciousness with the released energies in Space. It is the conscious cooperation with the energies of the stars that causes new cultures and civilizations to come into being.

In every age, there are two important factors to be considered: events and principles. Due to karmic debts, various painful events come into being. These events obscure our vision and discourage those who are constantly working to change world conditions through emphasizing the essential principles of Beauty, Goodness, Righteousness, Freedom, Joy, striving, and sacrificial service. Every time the cycle of destruction and corruption comes into

---

1. Please refer to *Cosmic Shocks* for additional information.

being, people feel that the power of principles is weakened and even destroyed forever. But they cannot see that these principles are immortal, and after any cataclysm, war or revolution, these principles radiate anew and once again bring health, happiness, success, prosperity, and enlightenment.

Thus, the real leader does not feel discouraged by the news of destruction, by the news of global corruption and jungle psychology. He knows that the broom of Life is in the process of cleaning, after which the principles will reappear in greater magnificence upon greater fields of human endeavor.

Thus ages come and go with their events, but the principles remain and show the path leading to new and higher achievements.

# 15

———•———

## *The Keynote of the New Age*

Those who are striving toward the New Era have a great vision in their souls.

Every New Era must be started with an accumulated tension for regeneration.

People in the world are sensing that a new life cannot be started with all the prevalent ideologies, religions, politics, educational systems, and national self-interests.

A new current of energy must penetrate into the spirit of humanity. What is that energy? That energy can be called the Energy of Synthesis which will penetrate into the seven major fields of human endeavor and create regeneration.

Close to the year 2000, the politics of the world must be regenerated by the idea of synthesizing humanity. Politics must offer to all members of humanity:

— freedom

— prosperity

— health

— happiness

The Energy of Synthesis must regenerate the education in the world, introducing the principle of unity — one world, one life — and the principle of responsibility. These should be the foundation for every educational project.

The Energy of Synthesis must regenerate the network of relationships everywhere in the world with the spirit of synthesis. Communication must be planned and people urged to actualize synthesis in the world through communication.

All arts in the world must strike the note of synthesis in their many and various expressions. Art must evoke the sense of essential unity latent in every heart, in every nation, in all humanity.

All themes of love, understanding, cooperation, sense of responsibility, freedom, and joy must strike the note of synthesis.

The science of the world must be put under the direction of responsibility. No invention and no discovery should be used to cause harm to Nature or to any living form. Science must work to demonstrate the basic synthesis of life and its forms.

The religions in the world must drop their antagonistic and separative spirits and seek to synthesize within them the most lofty concepts of human freedom, responsibility, joy, and communication with the Cosmic Intelligence. The religions of the world should bring the spirit of unity and synthesis into all their places of worship.

The world of finance should also synthesize the world, supervising the gifts of nature and labor, and distributing them under the light of unity and synthesis for all mankind so that each individual, country, and nation has all that is needed of food, clothing, and habitat; so that every person everywhere has the opportunity to expand his consciousness and manifest his talents and latent potentials to the degree that is possible.

Thus, the seven major fields of human endeavor will organize under the Spirit of Synthesis. Until the year 2000 and on the threshold of the New Creation, the most audible and impressive note will be *synthesis*. This note will be the leading vision for humanity. It is through this note that a new race will start to be born — equipped with the Spirit of Synthesis to alleviate all the ills of humanity, to restore joy and love and freedom, to bring health and integrity to the world. This new generation of leaders will introduce the Spirit of Synthesis in all fields of human endeavor. They will not manipulate the mind of humanity with horrible images of cataclysms but will talk about the victorious future of the human race.

This new generation will sound the note of righteousness in all nations, in all fields of human endeavor, to pave the way for the unity of mankind.

Righteousness will reinforce the three major laws in the Universe:

1. The Law of Economy
2. The Law of Attraction and Repulsion
3. The Law of Synthesis

*Righteousness* has a profound meaning. To be right or righteous means to be in harmony with the supreme note of Nature. If what you think, speak, and do are in harmony with that supreme note, you are righteous, as, for example, the notes of your musical instrument are not *right* if they are not tuned to the note of the tuning fork, or to the standard note.

The supreme note of the Universe is threefold:

— Beauty

— Love

— Light

Any thought that has beauty, love, and light is a right thought. Any word that is beautiful, full of love and light is a right word. Any action that has beauty, love, and light is a right action. If your thoughts have light and love but not beauty, your thoughts are not right.

What do beauty, love, and light do? Beauty relates you to all living forms and dissipates your separatism.

Love makes you feel responsible for the welfare of others.

Light shows you how to relate so that love and beauty are not violated.

Then these three aspects of the One Note, when operating, create *righteousness*.

Justice is based on man-made laws, or it is the result of agreement. If I agree with you that you must pay me ten dollars per hour, and you do not, you are violating our agreement, and you are not in justice. People create laws, and justice demands that you do not violate these laws. Righteousness is much beyond such a concept.

Righteousness means to be in harmony with the Note of the Universe, and the Note of the Universe is Beauty, Love, and Light. The closer you are to that Note, the better you express beauty, love, and light.

Beauty is power, will energy.

Love is compassion, understanding, harmony.

Light is knowledge of the things as they are.

All these three are the aspects of the One Note, the AUM. By striking the Note of the Universe and by tuning in our life and all our activities on all levels with that NOTE, we will bring in the Spirit of Synthesis. We will bring real and lasting joy, happiness, freedom, health, and prosperity to the world.

Every human being must do his best toward the year 2000 to actualize this vision.

At present, people are very fond of their computers because these provide services which meet their contemporary needs, in less time and in better ways. But there are important points that must be considered in relation to the computers and other machinery.

*The first point* is that all machinery, especially computers, emanate electromagnetic waves which may cause damage to the cellular electrical field of the body. This can have unexpected results and delay the evolution of humanity.

*The second point* is that machinery increases the time of labor. People have the fantasy that machinery will give them more time to follow their pleasures or spiritual pursuits. But machinery does the contrary; it increases your work hours and consumes more of your energy.

The pseudo-prophets told us that the more machinery we have, the more free time we will have. But you can now see that people are working more and have less time for themselves. The world is becoming a machine, and all human beings are becoming a part of that machine which is running day and night.

Go to the freeways of a big city and you will see the traffic flowing incessantly, day and night. Factories and offices of various kinds are open twenty-four hours. Most of the people in the world, especially in technologically

188 The Year 2000 & After

advanced countries, live in their cars. Airfields have no rest.
The machinery of the world is taking man hostage.

Of course, such pressures are affecting the mentality of
people, their health and relationships, and do not promise
a better future.

*The third point* is that the computer is becoming a tool
for totalitarianism. Every totalitarian establishment in all
fields of human endeavor will more successfully achieve its
goals through computers and other sophisticated devices.
These machines will serve them to impose their will more
easily on humanity.

This is a point that humanity must consider.

When our machinery serves our blind urges and drives,
our ego and vanity, and our separative interests, we become
its slaves — with related pains and sufferings.

When our consciousness expands and uses the machinery in a way that leaves us free, then the machinery
becomes our servant instead of our boss.

*The fourth point* is that the machinery consumes our
time and makes us depend on it. Such a dependence does
not give us a chance to develop virtues and work upon our
inner, divine potentials and then bring them out into expression.

There are great potentials within us which must manifest if we want more joy, more beauty, more freedom, and
of course more prosperity and the ability to enjoy them.

People do not understand that prosperity and success
are our enemies if we become slaves to produce prosperity
and success. We will lose the joy of life, the joy of freedom.

What are these potentials that must manifest from
within us if we want to evolve into a higher type of human
being?

Some of them are

1. Sense of responsibility

2. Cooperation

3. Goodwill

4. Inclusiveness

5. Beauty

6. Serenity

7. Peace

8. Gratitude

9. Contentment

10. Intuition

11. Direction

12. Sincerity

13. Creativity

14. Brotherhood

15. Synthesis

16. Understanding

17. Striving toward perfection

18. Ability to receive higher impressions

19. Telepathic communication

20. Sense of timing

21. Creative thinking

If these inner potentials do not manifest, they burn their containers like acid. The containers are our physical, emotional, and mental vehicles.

*The fifth point* is that machinery consumes nature and increases pollutants. It consumes the pure water, the pure ocean, the pure air, the pure atmosphere, and thus people live in an impure world in order to have machinery.

In the year 2000, people will consider the role of machinery in mental, emotional, and physical health. They will consider the impact of machinery on wars, in commerce, and they will propose simpler methods of living.

The year 2000 will be the beginning of the simplification of life. We will have less competition, more cooperation, more joy, and more free time. We will have less fear of authorities, less noise pollution, and less radioactivity and electromagnetic fields, the damages of which will be discovered in one hundred years.

The year 2000 can be a decisive year for humanity to choose between slavery, injustice, unrighteousness, and totalitarianism or freedom, righteousness, and real democracy — the foundation of which was heard in the words, "of the people, by the people, and for the people." Only on this foundation will a global life be constructed that prevents any nation or any group from ruling the destiny of humanity in a totalitarian spirit.

Toward the year 2000, people of the world will not accept slavery of any kind. Humanity will walk toward freedom — not toward independence. Humanity will learn the meaning of freedom and will see very clearly all those hindrances limiting its freedom. It will work to free itself from ignorance, from the dominion of selfish and destructive actions, negative emotions, separative thoughts, and from its past accumulated karma and harmful actions.

Harmlessness, freedom, joy, and beauty will be the four pillars upon which the new temple, the life of humanity, will be built.

For millions of years we have hated each other. We have fought, destroyed, and burned each other and each other's possessions.

For millions of years we have lived in separatism, in slavery, under the heavy control of the leaders of nations. The year 2000 is not a year but a gate of great opportunity beyond which people, for the first time, may touch their highest dreams of unity, peace, and synthesis.

We can have unprecedented beauty and joy after the year 2000. Inconceivable breakthroughs into Nature and the human mystery can be ours. Dear reader, arm yourself with the Spirit of Synthesis and let everyone see, hear, and feel the beauty of Synthesis as the keynote of the New Age.

The concept of synthesis will be assimilated and broadcast by those who have developed a new consciousness.

The New Era is the Era of Space. In the New Era, *Space Consciousness* will slowly grow and cause the disintegration of forms that have been crystallized in the spheres of our consciousness.

We will have a new understanding about the forms that are around us. They will be considered transient, temporary, illusive, and limiting. Not only the forms of tangible nature but also the forms of our emotions, the forms of our thoughts, knowledge, concepts, ideologies, beliefs — in brief, all that serves as the foundation of our lives and gives us protection and refuge — all these will slowly evaporate like mist in the canyons that rises to the sky and disappears.

Space Consciousness will slowly dominate our being and dissolve all our attachments to all the forms which we have worshipped and with which we have identified.

This will be the opportunity to discover our real identity and enter into the new dimension of Space Consciousness.

In the New Era we will be able to understand gradually the significance of freedom and joy, and our intuition will send higher rays into our mind to dispel all those forms which cause limitation, identification, pain, suffering, crime, and horror in many forms all over the world.

In one hundred year's time, Space Consciousness, or the consciousness that has the characteristics of non-identification with forms on all levels, will wipe out all the obsolete accumulation of imagination and fabrication in our mind.

Space Consciousness will let us understand that all forms are means to serve our emancipation and not means to keep us in slavery.

Such a new breakthrough to Space Consciousness will create responses and reactions.

Responses will create joy, freedom, and a new being-ness that is full of increasing potentials.

Reactions will create total confusion, aimlessness, and godlessness, which will result in inaction, depression, and even suicide.

The period of transition between the state of identification with form and Space Consciousness may bring turmoil in the world of mental, emotional, and physical life. Most people will feel that all is lost. But gradually, those who are responsive to the New Age consciousness will see the dawn of a new life.

These next few years can turn into a preparatory period for humanity to adjust itself to the challenges of Space Consciousness. If we respond to Space Consciousness, we will bring abundant freedom and joy, and in the meantime we will annihilate all objects of our attachment and separatism.

Do you realize through what pain and suffering the masses of people will pass, seeing the disappearance of all those forms which they have worshipped for ages and which have perpetuated their suffering?

Space Consciousness will wipe away all these *forms* which have obsessed us for millions of years.

Humanity allowed the weeds and jungles to grow around pure principles, enslave our spirit, and create an artificial life of ours and yours; a life of limitation, exploitation, totalitarianism, and slavery in all levels of our being and in all fields of human endeavor.

The emancipating spirit of humanity will no longer tolerate the mental, emotional, and physical slavery which has been imposing itself upon humanity and perpetuating the suffering and the illusionary happiness of the world.

What will be the effect of Space Consciousness upon our political, religious, and economic lives? The political ideologies will lose their meaning and significance and prove their failure. As a result, a new global political ideology will be formulated on the principles of non-exploitation, non-manipulation, non-slavery, and which is based on synthesis, unity, and freedom.

The religious doctrines and dogmas, claims, and fanaticism will slowly fade away in the increasing light of Space Consciousness. People will seek to contact the source of freedom and joy within themselves and within the Universe.

The economic life of the planet will be organized on the laws of sharing, non-competition, non-accumulation, and on the principles of circulation and service.

All economies have been used to gratify our personal pleasures, racial and national separatism and ego, to exploit other nations, and to destroy Nature. Money, so long worshipped, will serve as a source of energy to build a new humanity.

The leaders of the New Era who have acquired Space Consciousness will organize the economy of the world in such a way that there will be abundance, not waste, and not at the expense of Nature and man.

Space Consciousness will annihilate all limiting thoughtforms, all emotions that turn on the axis of the ego, all activities that cause harm and delay universal freedom.

The year 2000 is not far away. The disciples of the world are challenged to meet the ideals of the New Era, as were the wise virgins who kept their lanterns lit and thus were able to meet the Desire of all ages.

# Glossary

**Age of Aquarius:** The esoteric name given for the next cycle that we are about to enter, which is exemplified by universality and the expanded consciousness of man. Also known as the New Age.

**Ageless Wisdom:** The sum total of the Teachings given by great Spiritual Teachers throughout time. Also referred to as the Ancient Wisdom, the Teaching, the Ancient Teaching.

**All-Self:** That great Entity which pervades and sustains all things on all levels of existence.

**Archetype:** The original model from which all things of the same type are copied. The regenerative source of that type.

**Arhats:** Ancient term designating Fourth Degree Initiates.

**Ashram:** Sanskrit word. Refers to the gathering of disciples and aspirants which the Master collects for instruction. There are seven major Ashrams, each corresponding to one of the rays, each forming groups or foci of energy.

**Astral body:** The vehicle composed of astral substance, that through which the emotional aspect of humanity expresses itself. Also known as the subtle body and the emotional body.

**Atmic Plane:** See Planes.

**AUM:** Is translated as the energy of light, the energy of love, and the energy of directive will or power. It is the condensation of three fundamental Laws — the Law of Synthesis, the Law of Attraction, the Law of Repulsion.

**Aura:** The sum-total of all emanations from all the vehicles of any living thing.

**Bhagavad Gita:** One section of an epic poem called the Mahabharata. The story of the warrior-hero Arjuna — his conflicts, struggles, and his dialogue with his Inner Guide, Krishna. The story symbolizes the unfolding human soul at the transition stage toward Self-awareness.

**Center where "the Will of God is known":** See Shamballa.

**Central Life:** Also known as Central Magnet. The central Core of the Universe that pulls to Itself all Sparks in manifestation.

**Chalice:** Also known as the Lotus. Found in the second and third subplanes (from the top) of the mental plane. Formed by twelve different petals of energy: three love petals, three knowledge petals, three sacrifice petals. The innermost three petals remain folded for ages. They are the dynamic sources of these outer petals. The Lotus contains the essence of all of a person's achievements, true knowledge, and service. It is the dwelling place of the Solar Angel.

**Continuity of consciousness:** A state of consciousness in which you are aware on all levels of the mind and of the higher and lower planes simultaneously.

**Core:** The essence or spark of God within each being; the Monad.

**Corpse:** The shell of the astral or mental body which the human soul leaves behind after he passes into the mental plane, or the higher mental realms, respectively.

**Dark Forces:** Conscious agents of evil or materialism operating through the elements of disunity, hate, and separativeness.

**Dharma:** The exact location, the exact job, the exact position that you should be in.

**Disciple:** A person who tries to discipline and master his threefold personality, and manifests efficiency in the field where he works and serves.

**Divine Plane:** See Planes.

**Ego:** The human soul identified with the lower vehicles (physical, emotional, and mental) and their false values.

**Elementals:** The lives who operate the body they inhabit; three in number: physical elemental, astral elemental, and mental elemental.

**ELF currents:** Extra-Low Frequency electrical waves.

**Father's Home:** Shamballa, "the Center where the Will of God is known"; also, the Central Magnet.

**Fourth Initiation:** The Crucifixion Initiation during which the Solar Angel leaves and the Chalice is destroyed by the fully awakened Jewel or Core.

**Glamors:** Astral forms with a life of their own in the emotional body.

**Great Ones:** Beings who have taken the Fifth Initiation or beyond.

**Great Sages:** Also known as Great Ones. See Masters.

**Guardian Angel:** See Solar Angel.

**Hierarchy:** The spiritual Hierarchy, whose members have triumphed over matter and have complete control of the personality, or lower self. Its members are known as Masters of Wisdom Who are custodians of the Plan for humanity and all kingdoms evolving within the sphere of Earth. It is the Hierarchy that translates the Purpose of the Planetary Logos into a Plan for all kingdoms of the planet.

**Higher Planes:** See Higher Worlds.

**Higher Self:** Refers to the Solar Angel or Transpersonal Self.

**Higher Worlds:** Those planes of existence that are of a finer vibration of matter than the physical plane. Generally refers to the higher mental plane and above.

**Human soul:** See soul.

**Initiate:** A person who has taken an initiation. See also Initiation.

**Initiation:** The result of the steady progress of a person toward his life's goals, achieved through service and sacrifice, and manifested as an expansion of one's consciousness. It represents a point of achievement marked by a level of enlightenment and awareness. There are a total of nine Initiations that the developing human soul must experience in order to reach the Cosmic Heart.

**Inner Core:** See Core.

**Inner Guardian:** The Solar Angel.

**Inner Guide:** The Solar Angel.

**Inner Voice:** Also known as the "Voice of Silence." The Inner Voice is higher than the conscience. It is the Real Voice talking within you. It is direct communication with your Solar Angel.

**Inner Watch:** The Solar Angel.

**Intuitional Light:** When the emotional body is sublimated, it turns into a mirror that reflects the Divine Mysteries, the Divine Beauty, from the Intuitional Plane.

**Intuitional Plane:** See Planes.

**Karma, Law of:** The Law of Cause and Effect or attraction and repulsion. "As you sow, so shall you reap."

**Krishna:** The Teacher of the hero Arjuna in the *Bhagavad Gita*.

**Lower self:** The personality vehicles of the human soul. See also the self.

**Mantrams:** A prayer or invocation that, when repeated properly, produces real change in the person toward betterment, or a uniform orientation toward the goal of the invocation.

**Masters:** Individuals Who had the privilege to master their physical, emotional, mental, and Intuitional bodies.

**Mental Body:** The vehicle composed of the substance of the mental plane in which humanity expresses itself through thought.

**Mind, Higher and Lower:** See Planes.

**Monadic Plane:** See Planes.

**One Self:** The universal Life Soul pervading all existence.

**Permanent Atoms:** Each body of a human being has one permanent atom which is the archetype for the construction and constitution of that vehicle.

**Personality:** Totality of physical, emotional, and mental bodies of man.

**Plan:** The formulation of the Purpose of the Planetary Logos into a workable program — a Plan — by the Planetary Hierarchy for all kingdoms of nature.

**Planes:** There are seven planes through which a human being travels and which make up human consciousness. From the lowest level upward, they are called: Physical, Emotional or Astral, Mental, Intuitional or Buddhic, Atmic, Monadic, Divine. Each plane is subdivided into seven planes. The first three subplanes of the mental plane from the bottom are numbers seven, six, and five, which form the lower mental plane. Number four is the middle mind or link. Numbers three, two, and one form the Higher Mental Plane.

**Purpose:** That which the Solar Logos is intended to achieve at the end of the evolution of the Solar System. The Plan is the formulation of this Purpose for our planet only.

**Race:** The Ageless Wisdom divides human development into seven sections, called Root Races. From ancient times to the present, they have been called: Polarian Race, Hyperborean Race, Lemurian Race, Atlantean Race, Aryan Race, Sixth Root Race, Seventh Root Race. The latter two are the future states of human development. (For more information, see *Psyche and Psychism* by Torkom Saraydarian.)

**Rays:** See Seven Rays.

**self:** The small "s" self is the sumtotal of the physical, emotional, and mental bodies of man. Commonly called the "lower self" or personality.

**Self:** The capital "S" Self is another term used to refer to the Core of the human being. The True Self is the developing, unfolding human soul who is trying to liberate himself, go back to his Father, and become his True Self.

**Seven Departments of Human Endeavor:** The expression of the Seven Rays in human evolution, each corresponding to a specific Ray. They are: Politics, Education and Psychology, Philosophy, Arts, Science, Religion, Economics and Finance.

**Seven Rays:** These are the seven primary Rays through which everything exists. They are pure energy, vibrating to a specific frequency and condensing from plane to plane, from manifestation to manifestation. The three primary Rays or Rays of Aspect are: The First Ray of Power, Will, and Purpose; The Second Ray of Love-Wisdom; The Third Ray of Active, Creative Intelligence. There are four Rays of Attribute: The Fourth Ray of Harmony through Conflict; The Fifth Ray of Concrete Science or Knowledge; The Sixth Ray of Idealism or Devotion; The Seventh Ray of Synthesis or Ceremonial Order. These Rays indicate qualities that pertain to the seven fields of human endeavor or expression.

**Shamballa:** Known as the White Island, it exists in etheric matter and is located in the Gobi desert. Shamballa is the dwelling place of the Lord of the World, Sanat Kumara, and is the place where "the Will of God is known."

**Solar Angels:** Very advanced beings who sacrificed their life, descending from Higher Worlds to help the evolution of humanity and guide its steps toward initiation. This happened on our planet at the middle of the Lemurian period. They are also called Guardian Angels, or Flames.

**soul:** The small "s" soul is the human psyche, the Spark, traveling on the path of evolution and having three powers: willpower, attraction, and intelligence to guide its development. Also known as the evolving human soul.

**Soul:** Also known as the Solar Angel.

**Soul-infused personality:** A state in which the physical, emotional, and mental bodies are purified to a high degree and aligned with the Solar Angel so that the light of the Solar Angel can radiate through the personality in full power and beauty.

**Spark:** Human Monad fallen into matter.

**Spiritual Triad:** The field of awareness of the human soul. This field comes into being when the magnetic fields of the Mental Permanent Atom, the Buddhic Permanent Atom, and the Atmic Permanent Atom fuse and blend.

**Tara:** A female Master.

**Teaching, The:** See Ageless Wisdom.

**Third Initiation:** The total purification and alignment of the mental, emotional, and physical vehicles of the evolving human soul, leading to Transfiguration or Enlightenment.

**Three personality vehicles:** The three vehicles of man. The combined forces and vehicles in which the evolving human soul expresses himself and gains experience during incarnation. These vehicles are the physical body, the emotional or astral body, and the mental body.

**Tower, The:** See Shamballa.

**Transfiguration:** The result of the action of the electric fire of the Spiritual Triad on the Higher Mind. The lights in the little atoms of the personality vehicles are released, and the whole personality is purified in the Third Initiation.

**Transformation:** The result of the action of solar fire on the astral body. The astral body comes under the influence of the Solar Angel and the Intuitional Plane.

**Transpersonal Self:** The Solar Angel, the Inner Guide.

**Treasury, The:** Symbolic term for the Chalice.

**True Self:** See Self.

**Vanity:** Vanity is illusion based on egotistical pride of the personality. In essence, vanity is clothing an opinion of ourselves with a distorted perception of facts. It is a state of being wherein we think we are something which we are not; know something which we do not know; have something which we do not have; are able to do something which we are incapable of doing. It exists in mental matter in the aura and is fed by and through the personality.

**"Voice of Silence":** See Inner Voice.

**Wesak Full Moon:** Another name given for the full moon in Taurus. A ceremony, observed by people all over the world, focused on building a communication line to receive and pass to humanity the energy of spiritual will, love, and enlightenment. For additional information, see *Symphony of the Zodiac* by Torkom Saraydarian.

# Bibliographic References

Agni Yoga Society. New York: Agni Yoga Society.
   *Infinity,* vol. 2, 1957.

Bailey, Alice A. New York: Lucis Publishing Company.
   *The Destiny of Nations,* 1974.

Saraydarian, Torkom. Sedona, AZ: Aquarian Educational Group.
   *The Bhagavad Gita,* trans., 1974.
   *Hiawatha and the Great Peace,* 1984.
   *The Psyche and Psychism,* 1981.
   *The Science of Meditation,* 1981.
   *Sex, Family, and the Woman in Society,* 1987.
   *Symphony of the Zodiac,* 1988.
   *Woman, Torch of the Future,* 1980.

Saraydarian, Torkom. West Hills, CA: T.S.G. Publishing Foundation, Inc.
   *The Ageless Wisdom,* 1990.
   *Cosmic Shocks,* 1989.

# *Index*

## A

Abundance
  and exploitation, 150
Achievement, of others
  and regeneration, 160
Action
  and note of universe, 186
Age of Aquarius, 131
Age of person, 90
Age, designations of planet, 177
  real, defined, 177
Ageless Wisdom
  on killing, 128
Ages
  how formed, 180
All- Self, 62
All-compassionate, 63
All-inclusive, 62-63
All-loving, 63
All-sacrificial, 63
Anger, 9-10, 13-14, 23, 30-32,
  52, 56-57, 66, 69, 75, 79,
  84-85, 102, 108, 114, 123,
  125, 135, 142-144, 156, 176
Anger and year 2000, 10
Animosity
  as a current, 172
Appreciation
  in group formation, 45, 52
  spirit of, 45
  vs. respect, 46
Archetype
  and vision, 158
Arhat
  qualities of, 62
Arjuna, 132
Art
  and Law of Synthesis, 184
  and path of response, 149
Arts, 44, 69, 133, 143, 184
Arts, the
  for a better world, 130

Aspiration, 11, 14, 44, 135, 142,
  144, 158, 163
Astral body, 91
Astral body, global
  and effect of vices, 127
Astral World
  and result of killing, 128
Astronomer, 123
Atmic, Plane, 62
Attachments, 157
AUM, 187
Aura
  and habits, 106
  and illness, 125
  conditioning of, 20
Aura, human
  and Earth spheres, 125

## B

Beauty, 11, 13, 30, 34, 43,
  45-46, 48-52, 65, 69, 78-79,
  89, 91, 94, 96, 99-100, 108,
  112, 118, 124, 132-134, 137,
  149, 151-153, 157, 168, 176,
  180, 188-191
  and diplomacy, 172
  and joy, 159
  and New Era, 151
  and transformation, 99
  as a note, 186
  as a pillar, 190
Beingness, 112
  and sucess, 165
  defined, 103
Betrayal
  and group members, 72
Bhagavad Gita
  and dharma, 72, 81, 132
Blooming
  conditions for, 118
Bodies
  transformation of, 93
Bodies, higher
  and tuning in, 91
Bodies, three
  how to build, 89
Bodies, various
  and Higher Worlds, 150

Isolated Unity, 137-138
Isolation
    and retreat/meditation, 137

# J

Jealousy, 9-11, 13, 48, 56-57,
    66, 108, 113, 123, 125, 135,
    144, 176
    and other vices, 57
    and year 2000, 10, 79
    effect on bodies, 108
    how to be rid of, 57
Joy, 51, 53, 78, 82-83, 85, 106,
    108, 125-126, 135, 137, 140,
    150, 152, 156-159, 180,
    184-185, 187-188, 190-193
    and regeneration, 158-159
    and striving, 117
    and transformation, 99
    as a pillar, 190
    in New Era, 191
    of cooperation, 83
Justice
    defined, 186
Justification, self, 98, 100
    and Christ, 101

# K

Karma
    and calamities, 151
    and isolation, 137
    and killing, 127
    creation of, 63
Killing
    and Subtle World, 127
Knowingness, 103-104
Krishna, 81

# L

Labor, 160
    specific role in, 73

Laughter, 158
Law of Attraction and Repulsion,
    185
Law of Beauty, 132-133
Law of Cooperation, 133,
    139-140
Law of Economy, 174, 185
Law of Existence, 127-130
Law of Harmlessness, 132,
    134-135
Law of Karma, 162
Law of Love, 133, 142
Law of Purity, 132, 135
Law of Responsibility, 133, 140
Law of Right Human Relations,
    36
Law of Striving Toward
    Perfection, 133, 141
Law of Synthesis, 185
Law of Unity, 132, 136-137, 168
Law, Great, 59
Law, Universal
    and groups, 50
Laws, Cosmic
    violation of, 133
Laws, spiritual, 132
Leader
    and placement of people, 81
Leader(s), group
    how to improve, 45
    how to teach, 49
Leaders
    and Common Good, 150
    and group activities, 53
    and path of response, 148
    as victims, 175
    how to inspire, 43
    of the future, 193
Leadership
    and cooperation, 82
    and guiding oneself, 70
    defined, 43, 70
    duties of, 80
    foundation of, 71
    in year 2000, 185
    qualities needed, 77
    qualities of, 32
    where to start, 71

use of solar energy, 149
Sun-energy
  and colors, 150
Survival of the fittest
  defined, 10
Synthesis, 62, 135, 139,
  147-148, 183-185, 189, 193
  and year 2000, 185
Synthesis, Spirit of, 185, 187,
  191

# T

Talents, multi
  exposing of, 47
Teacher
  and discipline, 98, 101
  and Higher Self, 83
  and psychic energy, 107
  and regeneration, 160
  and Self, 96-97
  and self-justification, 100
  and Solar Angel, 97
  and standards, 113
  and striving, 112
  and Teaching, 101
  and transformation, 97
  duties of, 96
  effect on life, 102
  having one, 114
  how to find, 102
  on groups, 31
  role in building, 72
  role of, 66
Teacher, real kind, 97
Teaching, 109
  and children, 143
  how to, 81
  increase of, 23
Telepathic communication, 189
Television, 57, 130, 134-135,
  139, 141-143, 149
Television programs
  and cooperation, 139
Thinking, creative, 189
Thinking, free
  defined, 40
Thinking, pure
  defined, 135

Thought
  and note of universe, 186
Tibetan Master, 7, 15, 38, 69
Tornadoes, 128
Touchiness
  defined, 100
Tower, 147, 151
Transfiguration, 114
Transformation
  and beauty, 99
  and beingness, 104
  and change, 92
  and imitation of, 88
  and ownership, 112
  and reaction of bodies, 88
  steps of, 98
Transformation, defined, 87
Transformation, self
  steps of, 95
Transpersonal Self, 62
Transportation
  in future, 149
Treason
  and Teacher, 98
Treasury
  unlocking of, 79
True Self, 95, 100, 112, 116, 157
Truth, 31, 51, 80, 132
Tumors
  kinds of, 36
Twenty-first Century, 149

# U

Ugliness
  expression of, 133
Understanding, 171, 173, 189
Unit building
  as universal law, 33
United Nations, 33, 36, 78
Units
  and Universal Law, 35
  how to build, 42
  inhibitors of, 35
  qualities of, 34
  why create, 37
Unity
  defined, 136
  formation of, 36

# *Other Books by Torkom Saraydarian*

The Ageless Wisdom
The Bhagavad Gita
Breakthrough to Higher Psychism
Challenge for Discipleship
Christ, The Avatar of Sacrificial Love
A Commentary on Psychic Energy
Cosmic Shocks
Cosmos in Man
Dialogue With Christ
Flame of Beauty, Culture, Love, Joy
Hiawatha and the Great Peace
The Hidden Glory of the Inner Man
I Was
Joy and Healing
Legend of Shamballa
Other Worlds
The Psyche and Psychism
The Psychology of Cooperation and Group Consciousness
The Science of Becoming Oneself
The Science of Meditation
The Sense of Responsibility in Society
Sex, Family, and the Woman in Society
Spiritual Regeneration
Symphony of the Zodiac
Talks on Agni
Triangles of Fire
Unusual Court
Woman, Torch of the Future

*Vision Series Next Release:* **The Purpose of Life**

# Booklets by
# Torkom Saraydarian

A Daily Discipline of Worship
Fiery Carriage and Drugs
Five Great Mantrams of the New Age
Hierarchy and the Plan
Irritation — The Destructive Fire
Questioning Traveler and Karma
Spring of Prosperity
Synthesis
Torchbearers
Responsibility
The Psychology of Cooperation
Building Family Unity
The Responsibility of Fathers
The Responsibility of Mothers
What to Look for in the Heart of Your Partner

# About The Author

This is Torkom Saraydarian's latest published book. Many more will be released very soon. His vocal and instrumental compositions number in the hundreds and are being released.

The author's books have been used all over the world as sources of guidance and inspiration for true New Age living based on the teachings of the Ageless Wisdom. Some of the books have been translated into other languages, including German, Dutch, Danish, Portuguese, French, Spanish, Italian, Greek, Yugoslavian, and Swedish. He holds lectures and seminars in the United States as well as in other parts of the world.

Torkom Saraydarian's entire life has been a zealous effort to help people live healthy, joyous, and successful lives. He has spread this message of love and true vision tirelessly throughout his life.

From early boyhood the author learned first-hand from teachers of the Ageless Wisdom. He has studied widely in world religions and philosophies. He is in addition an accomplished pianist, violinist, and cellist and plays many other instruments as well. His books, lectures, seminars, and music are inspiring and offer a true insight into the beauty of the Ageless Wisdom.

Torkom Saraydarian's books and music speak to the hearts and minds of a humanity eager for positive change. His books, covering a large spectrum of human existence, are written in straightforward, unpretentious, clear, and often humorous fashion. His works draw on personal experiences, varied and rich. He offers insight and explanations to anyone interested in applying spiritual guidelines to everyday life. His no-nonsense approach is practical, simple, and readily accessible to anyone who is interested in finding real meaning in life.

Torkom Saraydarian has de-mystified the mysteries of the Ageless Wisdom. He has made the much needed link between the spiritual and the everyday worlds.

Look for exciting new books and music being released by Torkom Saraydarian.

# *Ordering Information*

Write to the publisher for additional information regarding:

—Free catalog of author's books and music tapes
—Information regarding lecture tapes and videos
—Placement on mailing list
—Information on new releases

Additional copies of *The Year 2000 & After.*
   U.S. $10.95
   Postage within U.S.A. $2.00
   Plus applicable state sales tax.

**T.S.G. Publishing Foundation, Inc.**
*Visions for the Twenty-First Century*
P.O. Box 4273
West Hills, California, 91308
United States of America